Ranjini Manian, Founder and CEO of *Global Adjustments*, is an inter-cultural coach to heads of multinational corporations and the Editor of *Culturama*, India's only culture magazine for expatriates. She founded the India Immersion Center and is the owner of the *globalindian* brand. She has lived in India, Japan and France. Educated in Mumbai University and Sorbonne Paris, she served on the Women's Leadership Board at Harvard.

Joanne Grady Huskey

Joanne Grady Huskey, Global Adjustments' Co-founder and North American Representative, is a cross-cultural trainer and international educator and has worked with many international companies in China, India, Kenya and Taiwan to assist their employees in transitioning to international living. Educated in Harvard and the University of Wisconsin-Madison, she is the vice-president of iLIVE2LEAD: Young Women's International Leadership Program. Part of a Foreign Service family, she has lived and worked in eight nations in Central America, Europe, Asia and Africa.

westland ltd
Make it In India

Together Ranjini and Joanne founded the company prophetically named *Global Adjustments*, twenty years ago, as India's premier expat mobility and cross cultural services firm.

They can be reached at *globalindian@globaladjustments.com*

Ranjini Manian is the author of:
Doing Business in India for Dummies
Upworldly Mobile
India Insights

Joanne Grady Huskey is the author of:
The Unofficial Diplomat

Make it In India
Global CEOs, Indo-US Insights

RANJINI MANIAN

and

JOANNE GRADY HUSKEY

𝓌

westland ltd

61, IInd Floor, Silverline Building, Alapakkam Main Road, Maduravoyal, Chennai 600095
93, Ist Floor, Sham Lal Road, Daryaganj, New Delhi 110002

First published by westland ltd 2015
Copyright © by Ranjini Manian and Joanne Grady Huskey 2015

ISBN
978-93-84030-84-1
Typeset by Ram Das Lal

The promise of a better tomorrow is not solely for Indians and Americans. It also beckons us to move forward together for a better world. This is the central premise of our defining partnership for the 21st century. Forward together we go — *chalein saath saath*.

President Obama & Prime Minster Narendra Modi OpEd in Washington Post.

DEDICATION

We dedicate this book to our Global Adjustments clients from 76 nations, who over the past two decades have asked us probing questions about India and the West, as they strive to be better global citizens.

We also dedicate this book to our two mothers, living in Chennai — India and Virginia — USA, who raised us to be free-spirited and open-minded agents of change.

CONTENTS

Foreword by N R Narayana Murthy

FOREWORD

N R Narayana Murthy,
Founder, Infosys

Henry Ward Beecher, a 19th century American Congregationalist clergyman, social reformer and speaker, once said, "Culture is that which helps us to work for the betterment of all." The world is becoming more globalized by the day. Interactions go beyond national boundaries. Cultural intelligence is important in everyday life. The avenues for greater trade relations between India and the US are becoming wider. We are going to have to work more closely together. It is important for both countries to carefully nurture and strengthen relationships.

At such a time, this book, **Make it In India** by Ranjini Manian and Joanne Grady Huskey, two women entrepreneurs who have twenty years of experience working with the two cultures and more, comes as a powerful instrument to help people of India and the USA achieve a comfortable and valuable working relationship.

Make it In India is a treasure house of many tips and facts. It contains, in an easy to read format, the wisdom of people who have had long years of hands-on experience. Men and women of India and the USA, who have led their respective business houses in successfully doing business with the other country, offer advice in friendly, day-to-day terms.

The tip that Phil Spender of Ford gives Americans: "As a Westerner, you have to be very patient and listen, and speak much less than in the West," may seem minor in the overall business context, but is really a very astute observation, because clarity of communication can make all the difference to business outcomes. When Kirthiga Reddy of Facebook says, "Go in active, not passive; don't say, 'They are going to tell me what they want me to do,'" it is something we Indians really need to ingrain in ourselves. Similarly, Zia Mody's (AZB & Partners) and David Sloan's (Eurasia Group, USA) inputs on tackling Indian bureaucracy are vital pointers to Westerners in negotiating this convoluted 'empire'.

Stuart Milne of HSBC Bank is giving sound advice when he recommends that people remain factual, neither overselling the India story nor underselling its challenges. Because we, in India, in our eagerness to portray our country in the best way, can overdo things, when actually, outsiders are aware of opportunities, but also want to know the risks.

Here's an anecdote from my own life: I was once on a train ride to Mantralaya and the man seated across from me started a conversation. By the second sentence he had asked me how his brother-in-law could get a job at Infosys. It made me realize how important it is for us as Indians to be friendly before becoming familiar with others.

Similar real-life experiences of the eleven CEOs in this book throw light on so much that is confusing, intimidating or annoying. Their sharp insights provide three overriding takeaways about interactions between America and India:

- Indians are thin-skinned. We see insults where none is meant. We really need to become more thick-skinned. On the flip side, Americans would do well to tone down their offhand comments.
- In India, we are uncomfortable facing unpleasant

situations. We do not like to communicate bad news. India – let us confront difficult situations and bring bad news to the table early and proactively. America – let us create a comfort factor to enable blunt speech.

- We Indians cannot say "No". We unquestioningly say "Yes" to whatever a client asks. So, Indians, do be honest in your promises, and Americans, do be open to probing more, and ensure that unvoiced concerns are addressed.

Besides helping each side to understand the other better, the business leaders interviewed in this book have also shown that there's much best business practice to learn from the other. Ranjini and Joanne have used their experience to draw from the CEOs nuances and little touches that can do so much to ease the passage on both sides.

The authors have also have shared their own insights on intercultural understanding, gained through running their company Global Adjustments, making many American companies successful in India and Global Indians successful in the world.

Overall, this book will, I'm sure, be a good reference point for both sides to acknowledge specific differences, evaluate their impact on business, and adapt or work around them to achieve the best possible results.

Make it In India is win-win. I wish you, as a reader, much success in the world.

INTRODUCTION

India has been attracting the world's attention for decades, but in recent years, it has become a major economic force recognized the world over. As a new Indian government rolls up its sleeves and gets down to work to steer the country to greater heights nationally and internationally, the world, in particular the USA, waits to engage with it. The two largest democracies in the world are on the verge of a new era of collaboration, in which culture-sensitive communication is going to play a big role — not only in the diplomatic context, but also in the economic and business scenarios. The way forward certainly lies in both sides appreciating what makes the other tick culturally and ideologically and learning to deal with it.

Still, to many in the West, India remains a land of mysterious rituals and strange working styles; while to as many Indians, the West's manners and values continue to be incomprehensible. Knowing a bit more about the rationale behind the other's behaviour could do wonders for easing the passage of today's global citizens, Indian and Westerner alike, and create a more lasting, compatible and cooperative relationship that will stand the test of time.

In this world of virtual reality and telecommuting, it no longer makes sense to cling to what one knows best and refuse to see the other viewpoint. One needs to make the effort to meet in the middle. In this book, *Make it In India,* we give you an opportunity to learn practical tips from the best of the best, and adapt quickly to today's global norms. Practical tips include key business topics such as running effective inter-cultural meetings, interacting from a position of strength during negotiations, managing multi-cultural team dynamics effectively, or optimizing the communication channels of a virtual workforce.

In *Make it In India* we present the wisdom of leaders both of the East and the West, men and women, CEOs who have led global teams successfully in India and the US. This wisdom of the trail prepares you the reader, from India, from the USA, or anywhere in the world for that matter, to work in multi-cultural teams with a renewed sensitivity to the other. The book offers the crystallized wisdom of global leaders, with Indian insights. It empowers the reader with armchair travel experiences of another's ways of thinking and behaving which are crucial to today's business success.

Tips from leaders in this book will positively enhance understanding of the other side and decrease potential social and business gaffes.

We, the authors, Ranjini Manian (an Indian) and Joanne Grady Huskey (an American), co-founders of *Global Adjustments*, India's premier re-locations firm, have had the opportunity for the past twenty years to work with business leaders from both eastern and western cultures. We started our relocation and cross-cultural business with the arrival of Ford Motor Company into India, as we acclimatized their first eighty global families hailing from countries as distant as Australia and Austria, Taiwan and Germany, Korea and USA, within Ford, to the Indian way of life and thinking. Over the years we have been a 'go to' India advisor for many Fortune 500 companies helping Foreign Direct Investment (FDI) to succeed in India. Managing Directors seek us out for messaging their speeches to State Governments, or for caring for their pets and for answers to the questions they had, from the sublime to the banal. And we have had the privilege of partnering with their entry and growth in the country.

As we mulled over the goodwill we had gathered for our nations, we realized that what made us successful was the ability to see the other's point of view while remaining rooted in our own value system. We looked around to see if there was a way for others to learn this quickly from world leaders. We found none in one place. The need for answers to questions repeatedly raised from both sides seemed imperative. How could we facilitate this with as many and as diverse a group in as short a time as possible?

And then the idea of this book emerged — a first on the bookshelf, it sets about explaining both viewpoints in one place, by global leaders with Indian insights. This book offers something brand new — a set of unique takeaways which springboards the reader into a global citizen, through the wisdom of twelve others who walked the trail before them.

To put together this book, we asked CEOs of top companies in India and the US questions that have come to mind frequently on both sides of the business divide, but have rarely, if ever, been publicly voiced to such high-level business leaders. The CEOs answered with insight and honesty, and peppered their advice with anecdotes. Eleven CEOs, from Facebook to Ford to Microsoft, shared with us tips and pointers they themselves have picked up along the way, both as individuals who adapted and bonded in the other's culture, but also as the experts they have become in cross-cultural business relations. They shared hard-hitting facts that lead to business improvements and make global business sense. And a twelfth man, a CEO par excellence, wrote the Foreword.

Make it In India addresses questions on a variety of subjects from both sides candidly. No other book that we know of does it this way. This book is a collection of real questions that real people, both Indian and American, have puzzled over while working with each other. It gives answers to the questions of one side, while pointing to those that the other side is struggling with. This book seeks to convey that adjustments are needed both ways. It shows that we are all human, and that with a little give and take in the short term, success can be assured for the long term.

If you are an Indian who interacts with Americans for business or study, or a US citizen, student, diplomat, or businessman, who lives and works in India or manages a virtual team, this book is for you! If you are a potential business partner from the US or from India, looking to expand your borders, this book is a great door opener to the universe of global business. And even if you are merely interested in academically equipping yourself as a global citizen, this book is a must for your reading list.

We founded *Global Adjustments* as a 'merger' between an American and an Indian. This merger has fuelled the company's growth to provide support and guidance to business people, Indian and Western alike, who are doing business in India.

As co-founders of *Global Adjustments*, we have interacted with seventy-six nationalities, enhancing their business success in India, and we have worked with thousands of global Indians to help them succeed in a multicultural world. The questions they asked us were revelations — and we have learned to listen to their questions and to find answers. *Global Adjustments* has been an India solutions provider for many MNCs in the emerging market. Our success is attributed to our utilization of the input of two cultures to solve new global issues. The fact that the CEOs, who we reached out to willingly shared their thoughts with us is a testimony to the value of the overriding theme of the book — that soft skills make hard business sense, and lifelong trade and friendships emerge if we base them on inter-cultural understanding.

We believe that today, more than ever, the merger of the best from both India and the US is what makes good business sense.

How to read this book

This is an easy-to-read book that can be dipped into anywhere, anytime, as a go-to for practical tips and for maximizing opportunities on both sides.

We have tried to create a user-friendly format. Each chapter has one lead-in question, which a selection of CEOs have answered. The rest of the chapter comprises separate questions on which one or more CEOs share their views.

Scattered through this book, you will find distinctive icons marking special snippets. One is titled '**It's a Fact!**' These are true-life anecdotes provided by the

CEOs themselves, to illustrate a point made in their answers, or simply, as self-explanatory answers.

The other is **Tips,** each identified by the name of the CEO who has provided it. For instance, you will find a tip from Ravi Venkatesan, former Microsoft Chairman, on how to manage the difference in time zones, and one from Sherry Murphree, former President, Dow Chemicals, on setting up 'buddy systems'.

We, the writers of this book and the founders of *Global Adjustments* have also reached into our repertoire to provide anecdotes and tips, based on our experiences and those of our staff over the years.

We hope this book will act as a catalyst for people from both cultures, enabling you to find out more about your own and others' cultures, for, it is in understanding that you are understood.

And one more thing before you go…

Think about this book as your unique private attendance at a celebrity dinner. They are no longer sages on stages that people are thronging to listen to. They become in this book, your guides by your side. How much there is to learn from each of them, and how they could precisely guide you in a very small period of time of networking is up to your application of the insight. Each answer provided by one CEO or another, by itself might give the initial feeling of being just a tit-bit. But wait till you reach the end of the meal and on your drive home, mull over the snippets you heard. You will see that you have learnt a great deal. Next, start applying these insights to your own situation. We are sure you will have many an 'aha' moment.

Happy reading and may you enjoy the process of adjusting to a new global community!

Ranjini & Joanne

MEET THE CEOs
(In order of their appearance in this book)

Ravi Venkatesan
Microsoft India — Former Chairman

This CEO was recently voted as one of India's best management thinkers by Thinkers 50. Making waves with his book *Conquering the Chaos: Win in India, Win Everywhere* published by Harvard Business School Press, Ravi crystallizes his experiences in formulae easy for others to follow.

As Chairman of Microsoft India between 2004 and 2012, Ravi helped build India into Microsoft's second-largest presence in the world and one of its fastest growing markets. He was instrumental in creating Microsoft India's *Project Shiksha*, a computer literacy programme which has so far trained over 40 million school children in India. Prior to Microsoft, Ravi was the Chairman of publicly listed Cummins India and led its transformation into a leading provider of power solutions and engines. He helped establish the Cummins College of Engineering, India's first engineering college for women, in Pune.

He is currently a Venture Partner at Unitus Seed Fund, which invests in early stage social enterprises. He is also founder and Chairman of Social Venture Partners India, a network of engaged philanthropists addressing social problems through venture philanthropy. Ravi serves on the boards of Rockefeller Foundation, Infosys and Strand Lifesciences. He has a B.Tech. from IIT Bombay, an MS from Purdue University, and an MBA from Harvard Business School, where he was a Baker Scholar.

Shanker Annaswamy
IBM India Private Limited — Former Managing Director

Among *India's 50 Most Powerful People* as listed by *Business Week 2009*, Shanker is known as a CEO who willingly shares his passion for excellence. He served a comprehensive geography, leading a large team as the Regional General Manager of IBM in India/South Asia (ISA) from 2004-2012.

Before joining IBM, Shanker was the President and Chief Executive Officer for GE Medical Systems, South Asia, and the Managing Director of Wipro-GE Medical Systems. He started his career with Philips Medical Systems.

He has held positions of eminence in several key industry forums. He was a member of NASSCOM's Executive Council from 2004 to 2008 and held the position of the Chairman of the CII National Committee of IP owners and co-chaired the Confederation of Indian Industry's National Innovation Mission in 2007. In 2009, he was nominated to the Prime Minister's Advisory Group on Science and Technology. He continues to be a member of the India @ 75 National Committee of CII. He also served as a member of the FICCI National Executive Committee and was on the National Executive Board of American Chamber of Commerce in India.

In 2011, Shanker was conferred the *Best CEO — Multinational Company Award* as part of *Forbes India Leadership Awards 2011 for Transformational Leadership.*

Zia Mody
AZB & Partners, India — Founder and Senior Partner

This *Outstanding Women Business Leader of the Year — 2013* awardee at *India Business Leader Awards* is greatly admired for her spot-on legal advice combined with a human touch.

Zia Mody is one of India's foremost corporate attorneys. Educated at Cambridge, and then Harvard, this member of the New York State Bar began her career at Baker & McKenzie, New York. Five years later she moved to India to set up practice, establishing the Chambers of Zia Mody, which became AZB & Partners in 2004.

Listed by *Forbes India (2013)* as one of *India's 10 Most Powerful Women* and by *Forbes Asia* as one of *Asia's 50 Power Businesswomen* (2012), Zia has vast experience in acquisitions, joint ventures, company restructuring, foreign inward investment related practice and corporate law.

Her abilities are recognized globally, as is reflected in her appointment as a Non-Executive Director of the HSBC Asia Pacific Board, member of the World Bank Administrative Tribunal, Washington DC (2008-2013), and Vice-President and Member of the London Court of International Arbitration (2010-2013). Zia serves on various advisory committees of the Confederation of Indian Industry and on the Committee on Corporate Governance constituted by the Ministry of Corporate Affairs. She was nominated to be part of the 'Committee on Rationalisation of Investment Routes and Monitoring of Foreign Portfolio Investments' formed by the Securities and Exchange Board of India. Zia is a member of the Godrej Committee on Corporate Governance, recently constituted by the Ministry of Corporate Affairs, and of the Reserve Bank of India Committee on Comprehensive Financial Services for Small Businesses and Low-Income Households.

Among her many awards, is the *Legal Icon of the Decade, 2013* award at the *Legal Era Awards*.

Jukka Lehtela
Nokia — Former Director, India Operations

Warm, vibrant, an India–US business partner, a telecom engineer by education, a global nomad by experience, Jukka has spent most of his career working with Nokia. He has held different positions in the areas of Sourcing, and Supply Chain Management and Manufacturing. During his various assignments, he has been stationed in the US and in India and worked with many cultures around the world. During his assignment as Director, India Operations, Jukka's task was to establish a manufacturing unit in Chennai, Tamil Nadu, with surrounding supplier factories. This *Special Economic Zone* was built in 2005 in record time and has manufactured hundreds of millions of phones. At the Nokia factory in India, Jukka headed a 10,000 strong Indian workforce and the total headcount at the Special Economic Zone which also housed supplier factories was around 40,000.

He has had two stints in the US. The first (1989-1990) was in Florida, where he worked for the Nokia Sourcing office. From there, he moved to San Diego to establish sourcing activities for a new R&D center (1990-1992). As Vice-President, Supplier Integration, at Nokia Mobile Phones, Jukka developed and implemented a supplier-owned inventory model; as Head of Procurement, Nokia Networks, he led a team of 1000 Procurement Experts and helped the company achieve significant business savings.

After his stint in India, he returned to Finland. The positions he has held include CPO for Vaasan Oy, an industry-based company, and VP, Global Sourcing, for Fiskars, an internationally known metal and consumer brands company based in Finland.

Kirthiga Reddy
Facebook India — Managing Director

One of *Fortune India's 50 Most Powerful Women in India*, Kirthiga is a most unassuming yet dynamic leader of a new age, game-changing company. Kirthiga leads the Global Marketing Solutions teams in India and plays a key role in building and maintaining strategic relationships with top regional agencies and clients. She joined as the first Facebook India employee in July 2010 and set up the India operations in Hyderabad, supporting the company's growing number of users, advertisers and developers worldwide.

Prior to Facebook, Kirthiga was VP and GM of SaaS-based Consumer Security business unit and India operations at Phoenix Technologies. She led a global team located in the US, India, Japan, Korea, and Taiwan. Kirthiga has also held the position of Director of Product Management at Motorola, Director of Engineering at Silicon Graphics, and Associate at Booz

Allen Hamilton, with most of her professional life based in Silicon Valley, California.

After qualifying as a Computer Engineer from India, she went on to do an MS at Syracuse University and holds an MBA from Stanford University, graduating with top honors as an Arjay Miller Scholar.

It is not surprising that Kirthiga has been featured as *Fast Company's 100 Most Creative People in Business 2013, Business Today's hottest young executives* and *Impact's 100 Icons of India Digital Ecosystem* among other recognitions. Kirthiga is also the Vice-Chairman of the Internet and Mobile Association of India (IAMAI). She is passionate about causes for children and about developing women leaders.

Stuart Milne
HSBC Bank India — CEO

A New Yorker by residence and marriage, and an India aficionado, Stuart Milne brings his incisive banker insights to our questions. Stuart is Group General Manager and Chief Executive Officer for HSBC's business in India, one of HSBC's key priority countries globally. He was appointed to this role in February 2012, prior to which he spent five years as Chief Executive Officer for HSBC Japan. He is a member of HSBC's Executive Committee for the Asia Pacific Region.

During his thirty-three year career with HSBC, Stuart has worked in the USA, France, Japan, Hong Kong, Philippines, UAE and Bahrain, as well as India, in a wide variety of roles. He was born in Kirkuk in northern Iraq. His father was an oil industry executive and his grandfather a British Army officer who served in Iraq during the First World War. Stuart is active in the business community and serves as Chairman of the British Business Group of Mumbai.

R K Krishna Kumar
Tata Starbucks — Former Chairman

Awarded the *Padma Shri*, a national honour, by the President of India in 2009 for his contribution to the growth of Indian industry and trade, R K Krishna Kumar is an iconic figure at Tata Industries. His is a greatly respected name in Indian business circles.

He joined the Tata Administrative Services in 1963 after a Masters in Politics and Public Administration from the Madras University and was appointed to Tata Industries. Over the past fifty years, Krishna Kumar has been a key executive with the House of Tata, and has served in several Tata Companies in various capacities.

He was a Director of Tata Sons Ltd., the holding Company of the Tata Group, and Director on the boards of many Tata companies. He was Vice-Chairman of Tata Global Beverages Limited and the Indian Hotels Company Limited, and Chairman of Tata Coffee Ltd., Infiniti Retail, TRIL and THDC. It was under his leadership that Tata Starbucks came into being.

He is currently a Trustee of the Sir Dorabji Tata and Sir Ratan Tata Trust. He is the Trust's Nominee on the Governing Council of Tata Institute of Fundamental Research and the Court of the Indian Institute of Science.

Kiran Mazumdar-Shaw
Biocon Limited — Chairman & Managing Director

Among *TIME Magazine's 100 most influential people in the world*, Kiran Mazumdar-Shaw is known for her plain speaking and intuitive intelligence. She is admired as a pioneer of the biotechnology industry in India, and is the Chairperson and Managing Director of India's leading bio-pharmaceuticals company, Biocon. She has made her country proud by harnessing the power of biotechnology through affordable innovation to make world-class therapeutics accessible to patients around the globe. Under her stewardship, Biocon has evolved since its inception in 1978 from an industrial enzymes company to a fully-integrated, innovation-led, emerging global biopharmaceutical enterprise committed to reducing therapy costs of chronic conditions like diabetes, cancer and autoimmune diseases. Recently, US based Chemical Heritage Foundation conferred her with the *2014 Othmer Gold Medal* and Germany-based *Kiel Institute for the World Economy* awarded her its coveted *2014 Global Economy Prize for Business*.

Philip G Spender
Ford Motor Company — Former President, India

Phil is a leader who has now left India, but in whose heart India remains. An Automotive Industry Executive with extensive global experience in general management and joint ventures, he has led large diverse workforces at Ford Motor Company in six different countries. He is now retired and serving on company boards and consulting with Jaguar Landrover in the UK and their Chery Landrover Joint venture in China,

He served on eleven boards in India, USA, China, Japan and Australia as a Director, Representative Director, and Chairman, including at Ford India, Mahindra Ford JV, and Mahindra & Mahindra.

Born and educated in New Zealand, he joined Ford in 1975 as an engineer and served in a variety of engineering, finance and management roles until 1985 when he moved to Ford Australia for thirteen years.

Phil served Ford in India, USA, China, and Japan in senior leadership roles and as Corporate Vice-President and company officer, launching the 2005 Mustang and opening up the new markets of India as Managing Director. While in India, Phil commissioned the Chennai plant and launched and grew the new company. He played an active role in the Society of Indian Automobile Manufacturers (SIAM) became a life member of the Madras Motorsports Club and received the *For the Sake of Honour* award from *Rotary Club* for services to Indian motorsport and the community.

Sherry Murphree
Dow Chemical Company — Former President,
India Engineering Center

An active advocate of diversity, in what was once a male-dominated industry, Sherry Murphree has spent her career as an engineer and leader in the petrochemical industry. Her thirty-one year career has been in Manufacturing, Engineering, Purchasing and Information Technology for the Dow Chemical Company.

Outside of the United States, the biggest centre was established in India by Dow in 2006. She served here as the first President of the India Engineering Center which Dow set up in Chennai, South India.

Sherry received her BS in Industrial and Systems Engineering from Auburn University. She now lives in Houston, Texas. After a high-achieving career, Sherry is now active as a volunteer with MD Anderson Cancer Center, working with cancer patients and also with Child Advocates working with children in foster care.

David Sloan
Eurasia Group, USA — Practice Head, Asia,
Area of Expertise: India

An Indian in an American skin or an American with an Indian mindset, David gracefully moves from one culture to the other in his leadership journey.

As the Practice Head for Asia with the Eurasia Group, David Sloan primarily focuses on India, with particular emphasis on political developments that affect global companies and investors. An India specialist since 1988, he also develops and helps implement market entry and business development strategies, identifies and vets potential business partners, and helps resolve commercial disputes and other corporate problems. His sectoral expertise includes the energy and power, financial services, infrastructure, defense, retail, and telecommunications industries.

Prior to working at Eurasia Group, David was The

Scowcroft Group's senior consultant for South Asia for seventeen years and president of Corporate Strategies International. He previously served as Executive Vice-President at Charles Percy & Associates, a Washington-based international consulting boutique, and before that, was an economic officer in the US Foreign Service for eight years. David has also been a Fellow at the American Enterprise Institute in Washington and the Rajiv Gandhi Institute in New Delhi. His articles on South Asia and various international topics have appeared in the op-ed pages of the *New York Times*, *Los Angeles Times*, *Asian Wall Street Journal*, *International Herald Tribune*, and *Times of India*, among other publications. He has served on the boards of both private and publicly traded companies as well as on the boards of a number of international NGOs. David holds a BA (cum laude) from Tufts University and a MALD from The Fletcher School of Law & Diplomacy.

FIRST CONTACT

*"You never get a second chance to make a first impression," goes a popular saying. This chapter will give you some clues about how to make that first contact between an American and an Indian business person go well. The desired result is to meet the expectations of courtesy on both sides, and, hopefully, for the first meeting to lead on to several more. People like to do business with people who are **like them**, or with people they **like**. In this chapter, CEOs give insights on how an American can be well received from the word go by an Indian, and how the Indian can make that first meeting with an American, one that builds a lasting relationship. Going step by step, from appearances, through body language, forms of address and conversation, to gift-giving, and ending with overall first impressions, this section offers a starter kit to sailing through that crucial initial meeting.*

Hit the ground running
Photo: Global Adjustments, India

How can Indians and Americans make a positive first impression on one another?

Ravi Venkatesan, Microsoft India

I went to the US in 1985, when I was twenty years old, I had no money, and Indians were not as abundant as they are today. I used to be one of only two Indians in a large group, and I had to fit in. What I discovered, as a person coming into any dominant culture, is that it is extremely important to be humble, because you don't know enough.

The second ingredient is to have curiosity about the other and learn from the word go.

Thirdly, do be authentic — don't be apologetic. I have no respect for Indians who develop a twangy accent. There is no point in being unnatural. Don't try to be something you are not, and the first impression will lead to many more successful layers in business.

Tips from...

Global Adjustments

Prepare an 'Elevator Speech'. Write down in 50 words or less, who you are, and what you do, and practice saying it, so that it comes out naturally when you meet anyone for the first time. Even if it is the President of the United States or the Prime Minister of India you have to be ready with an interesting pitch — and all you have is the time it takes for an elevator (or 'lift' as it is called in India) to get from the 20th floor down to earth . This elevator pitch can really take you places!

Shanker Annaswamy, IBM India

In my career spanning over thirty-six years, I was fortunate to work for almost a decade each in three great global companies — Philips, GE and IBM. In all the three companies there were opportunities for employees to work with colleagues of different cultural backgrounds and at different locations across the world.

Generally, most of the companies train their employees on soft and communication skills. From my learning and experience, I would focus on the following three areas:

a. **Always prepare** — As they say, the first impression is the best impression. Apart from preparing for the meeting objectives, it would help to know about the educational/technical/cultural background of the person. Knowledge of the person's language, hobbies and other interests helps to build some connections.

b. **Speak slowly** — Most of us from India speak fast and our accent varies depending on the region we come from. It would help immensely if we speak clearly and slowly in a measured manner, so that the other person understands us better.

c. **Listen actively** — For some of us, our listening skills are not the best! Our minds tend to wander off to the next topic after we ask a question, instead of listening and paying attention to the speaker.

Zia Mody, AZB & Partners, India

A large number of our clients are American and our younger lawyers observe other experienced partners in the firm as they engage in negotiations with Westerners for the first time. Our engagement with American clients has to be quite frank, quite upfront in what our advice is. We try not to leave things unsaid or have anything lost in translation. Americans are an open set of very transparent people, and my impression of them is that they want to get very quickly to what they call 'the bottom line'. Therefore, although you can nuance the advice/message with an American client, you have to get to the point quickly.

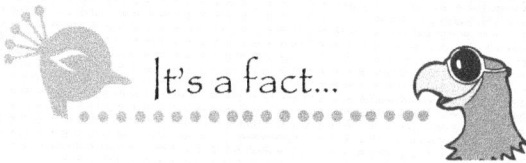

It's a fact...

Loud negotiations with combative posturing, by one of my clients, really delayed the signing of a deal, in the case of one important acquisition in which we assisted. We had to advise the Indians on the other side that it was done unintentionally and was actually an indication of the long-term commitment of our Western client, who intended to be a true long-term partner to them. God knows if they believed it, but the deal was signed!

– Zia Mody

Jukka Lehtela, Nokia

This is not just about first impressions one way, but about impressing each other overall and being understood. We never had an expat and India team divide in our company. Our team was big, everyone was responsible for their own area. One thing we did do was to use non-resident Indians, who understood both sides, to translate what the Indians really meant when they spoke.

Tips from...

Zia Mody

For the American clients who come to work with Indians, the advice we give them is "Indians are not always direct and frank. They are not confrontational. They will try to postpone any unpleasant discussion or bad news for later. Therefore, especially in a joint venture, it is very important, that in a nice way, all the points are brought to the table, so there are no surprises later." Nobody should say "I thought it would be this — not that." We also advise American clients to be sensitive to Indian culture — hugging women or unintentionally being over-friendly should be toned down in the beginning, at least until you become friends.

Kirthiga Reddy, Facebook India

There are often opportunities for our Facebook teams to hold one-on-ones with key players on both sides, and they come out and say, "I don't know if I really used that one-on-one very effectively." My advice has always been to go in with a message, take the time to put your thoughts down about what is it you want the other person to leave with. Think of the areas of challenge you have, and think about places this person can help — especially visitors from headquarters. Everyone is eager to help and make a difference. Most of all, stay true to the business and the intent, don't go down the path of visibility for visibility's sake, because people can see through that.

Tips from...

Global Adjustments

Getting names right is a fun challenge. Western names are best remembered written down, then practiced so that they are pronounced right.

For instance, we needed to put an effort into remembering that our VIP client Bezos's name was pronounced "Bay-Zos" and not "Bee-soz." Among Indian names, the top businessman Nandan Nilekani's name was one spelling we repeatedly got wrong until we were able to link it with the river "Nile". For the Western ear, some Indian names are too complicated to remember – one like Jayakrishna Hariharan, for instance. In such cases, breaking them down into syllables makes it a little easier. Or simply reduce it to initials – JKH, after seeking permission from the person concerned, as he or she will willingly oblige.

Stuart Milne, HSBC

One of the things I recommend to my people, who have internal and external meetings, is that they remain factual, not to oversell the India story and not undersell the challenges that India faces. Sometimes, Indian colleagues can push the India story too much, when actually, outsiders are aware of opportunities, but also want to know the risks. It is about coming across as somebody who has something useful to say, not regurgitating a line, but giving useful advice.

As bankers, we often advise customers on strategies to execute, to succeed despite the idiosyncrasies that exist. Broadly speaking, there tends to be a lot of talk, but translating it into action is harder. I advise foreigners coming here that they won't find a more intelligent bunch of people than Indians anywhere — very motivated to succeed — but at the same time everybody wants to be the chief and not everyone is as focused on execution. Going from cool strategy stuff, to bringing them down to earth to execute, has to be incorporated into the leadership mentoring style of expats coming to lead teams here.

Tips from...

R Krishna Kumar

When you begin a genuine conversation with cultural understanding, taking interest in the person and his way of life, it will flow much smoother into business discussions in the company.

Kiran Mazumdar-Shaw, Biocon Ltd

We deal with senior company officials, reputed scientists and visiting business delegations very often. Of course first impressions matter, which is why both sides need to be well presented in appropriate professional attire. Naturally, soft skills coaching is a must, along with the right greetings, proper handshakes, and knowing how to behave at restaurants, order food, and speak up confidently.

Tips from...

Kirthiga Reddy

One of my early mentors told me, "Kirthiga, I want you to focus on the clients that we serve, the success of the organization you are part of, and the success of the team you belong to. If you do those three things, your success will be the by-product." It is an empowering philosophy that has stayed with me. Therefore, go in active, not passive, don't say, 'They are going to tell me what they want me to do." Go in armed and ready.

Phil Spender, Ford Motor Company

As a Westerner, you have to be very patient and listen, and speak much less than in the West.

You have to summarize what you think you have heard.

Then, take the time to repeat back to them what you heard, looking around the room to ensure that's what people meant to say.

As a leader in a foreign environment, you have to make yourself available to all levels, walk the plant and keep yourself available, give key messages early on.

You have to be very clear, and also you have to be firm.

You have to respect Indian beliefs and protocol and be willing to learn, balancing this by utilizing what you know is global best practice.

It's a fact...

There was this tree on the land where the Ford plant was built, which truthfully speaking would have to be cut down to level the ground to get the most optimum lay of the land for the factory construction. We didn't realize, however, that it was a sacred tree, a banyan. Before we knew it, the whole village knew about this, and was up in arms. We dialogued with them, and assured them that the banyan tree would be preserved, and even, eventually, became the focal point of the factory. I had seen Ford model Ts photographed under banyan trees, when Ford was in India many years ago, so the banyan tree was meaningful then, and remains meaningful now.

– Phil Spender

How do I understand terms like business casual and business formal, so that I dress the right way and make a good first impression?

Sherry Murphree

People need to feel free to ask what one should do in any situation. I want to encourage Indians to ask questions; all concerns are fine. You don't have to ask your boss, but, find a peer to confer with.

We made no distinction between men and women, professional dress meant what we both wear to work in the US. At Dow in India, it was perfectly suitable for women to wear *kurtas* with their jeans, if they wanted. They just had to ask to find out the right dress for the right time.

Tips from...

Global Adjustments

Business casual means collared shirt, formal trousers and shoes and belt matching each other. Business formal mostly means a suit and tie added on.

Colours of suits are usually solid dark shades, and browns are best avoided. Narrow pin stripes on suits are elegant, and ties of solid colour or small designs are a good accessory. Well-polished shoes, well-groomed hair, and a well-kept leather bag are image enhancers. Grooming oneself from hair to nails, and ensuring that one smells pleasant, are all a part of making a good first impression. Attention to details like buttoning down Oxford shirts, if you wear the kinds with buttons on the collar, and not leaving them flapping, will go towards creating a meticulous look. Women can be in formal Western suits or Indo-Western wear, with minimal jewelry, following the concept of 'less is more'.

Should Westerners dress in Indian attire while doing business in India?

David Sloan, Eurasia Group

Westerners are admired for their own professional look actually. There are big differences in what business people wear in Bombay and Delhi. Dress in Delhi is much more conservative and people wear suits more than in Bombay. Chennai and Bangalore are also quite different too. Bangalore has become quite Western and Chennai is relaxed with shirt and formal trousers.

It's a fact...

I went to Gwalior, a city of one million, with a group from the US Embassy, who you would think would know better. At the special event we attended, some of the Embassy women were wearing tank tops and other inappropriate clothing. Some of the younger Indian males responded by pinching the women, who in turn, screamed in protest. The situation became quite ugly and could have been avoided, if they had taken culture into consideration when dressing.

– David Sloan

Dressing Indian style is done more by Western women than Western men, and can be fine, depending on how good the women can make themselves look. I would certainly not advise dressing like a local at a higher organizational level, but, if a person is known for having a taste for Indian culture, that may be more acceptable in informal settings. The important point is not to pander to audiences or go overboard.

Kiran Mazumdar-Shaw, Biocon Limited

Actually, it is really not by dress alone that we are judged — it is important to fit into the scenario in India or overseas but there is no need for a Westerner to wear Indian attire. At the end of the day, you are judged by how you conduct yourself and the knowledge you have. On the flip side some Indian women prefer to wear a sari overseas for business meetings, while others are more comfortable with Western attire. I find it comfortable and easy to wear more Western formal business wear. Everyone has to find their comfort zone.

What would be an icebreaker conversation to use when Americans and Indians meet for the first time?

R K Krishna Kumar, Tata Group

When I interact with American leaders, especially when they come to India and want to understand, I play the role of a Cultural Ambassador. A good icebreaker is explaining Indian tradition and roots in a simple format. Expats have a very different view, they only know of our vast population and old fashioned ways. They see us as a country full of godmen, and it is up to us to explain the basis of Indian culture. I explain it in three layers: what you see — maybe holy men and orange robes; the ritualistic side of temples and holy places; and the third layer, which is the symbolism behind these, which is quite logical. It is this world of spirituality where India's fountainhead of meaning springs up and gives us our world-renowned inherent strength. This makes for an interesting conversation starter with Americans, who admire ancient civilizations. One needs to speak up for India.

When you go overseas, it is important to know enough to talk about what makes those cultures tick, the location-specific mores and behaviour and to understand their cultural fountainhead. It breaks the ice if we take genuine interest in one another's way of life.

Technology is bringing so much power virtually, geographies are no barriers to entry into mindsets at all.

At a business meal, as I am concerned about health, how can I, as a Westerner, politely refuse the excessive food and drink offered?

Krishna Kumar

Indians do tend to offer a lot of food and drink and not offer a lot of explanation with it. So it is understandable if this flummoxes you. Do feel free to ask, for example, if it is mineral water; apologetically say you are unable to eat too much due to jet lag or travel; and acknowledge your lower immune systems openly. Take a little of the food offered, and if you take seconds of anything it will leave your Indian host delighted.

If you are an Indian host, remember, expats need to be given space. Indians need to lay it out and explain unique foods, but don't push it down on the expatriate.

Encourage it, but don't worry or be sensitive to his or her partaking of it. Offer healthy food options, and announce the ingredients. The world is becoming conscious about this aspect these days. It is all give and take, and both sides simply need to pick up cues. It all boils down to respecting individual choices.

Tips from...

Global Adjustments

If you are an American guest, feel free to ask what ingredients have gone into something. Be ready to be asked multiple times to partake of food and drink. Vocalize politely your willingness to try out different foods, and explain your inability to partake of some.

At a business meal, how can an Indian hold his or her own as a vegetarian teetotaler?

Krishna Kumar

So long as you don't have an inferiority complex, it is never an issue. I have seen senior leaders in Europe and the US, who respect your sense of dignity and purpose.

So just hold your own. Don't be defensive. Your personal preference is your own. It doesn't make you any higher or lower. In the US too, people are choosing to be vegetarian or even vegan (no meat or dairy) so, the concept is more accepted these days. Sip juice or club soda while others drink a glass of wine. Learn to relish a salad and sandwich as a vegetarian and not be stuck on hot look-alike Indian food.

Indians don't use first names easily. They address seniors as 'Sir' or add the suffix 'Ji' to their name. How do I explain to the American not to take this as bureaucracy or being overly formal?

Shanker Annaswamy

In India, based on regional and cultural practices, it is common to address seniors as *Sir* or *Ji*, even if we have known them for many years and have close relationships. In America, in similar situations, people would like to be addressed by their first name.

The common error Americans make is to judge someone else calling me Mr. Annaswamy as a reflection of a hierarchical management style, while it is merely a simple form of address here in India. It does not necessarily mean that by calling someone by their first name you are closer, or by addressing them as *Sir* or *Ji* you are extremely formal.

Jukka Lehtela

This is kind of a personal thing for people. In our country, we prefer to be called by Mr. or Ms. and our last name for formality. Jukka was how they (in India) usually referred to me, but, I didn't care about this informality too much, I understood that they would be formal out of respect when needed. And that they would always be more formal to older Indians than me.

What gifts can I take to establish a warm and friendly atmosphere right at the beginning?

Sherry Murphree

Bring small gifts of candy, a calendar or planner with scenery from your country, or even a music CD. Indians could carry a decorative sandalwood elephant for the office table and Americans might carry a photo frame with Americana back to India, but make sure they are not expensive items, because large gifts can be construed as bribery, although it may not be intended as such. Most companies have rules and limits about accepting gifts.

 It's a fact...

Just like Christmas which is a time for giving, in India Diwali is an important time to acknowledge the contribution of people by giving bonuses or gifts. Starting from a driver who serves you, to a VP in your company, a Diwali bonus is mandatorily part of the cost to company package to be taken into account. Add-ons of boxes of sweets or earthen lamps (traditional tokens of good luck for the festival of lights, which is Diwali), will be greatly appreciated. In the West, birthdays are considered personal information. And wedding anniversaries are most private. Unlike this, in India, people know and acknowledge each other's special commemorative days. An expat once shared with us the story of how she presented a simple box of Lindt Chocolates to a crucial player on her Indian team on his wedding anniversary. After he shared the gift with the rest of the team, he confessed to her that he had been on the point of putting in his resignation, thinking that his work wasn't really valued, but the fact that she had remembered his special day had changed his whole perspective! He was motivated to work even harder.

– Global Adjustments

CHAPTER 2

MEETING EXPECTATIONS

This chapter provides replies to questions that have been buzzing in our heads both ways, as we set up bi-cultural meetings. Whether in personal meetings, or virtual video/teleconferences, each culture wishes they could understand why the other does things so differently from them. Basically, in India, meetings are meant for information sharing by a senior person from whom others can learn. In America, however, meetings are places to put your best ideas forward, to brainstorm and solve issues, to set your own goals, and show others how you will achieve them. This difference in intention is to be kept in mind, as we look at the answers provided by our consortium of CEOs, who have shared insights about holding successful meetings.

Shared Focus
Photo: Brigitte Rhodius, UK

How have you adjusted meeting protocol in order to manage meetings with multi-cultural teams?

Ravi Venkatesan, Microsoft India (former Chair)

To me, there are simply good meetings vs. bad meetings in either culture — the absence of protocol results in bad meetings.

1. It is helpful to have an agenda. Be clear about what outcomes you hope to arrive at. Start on time and end on time. Wandering in after the first fifteen minutes seems common in India, while five minutes is common in the US. People should not have to waste time trying to find out where you are.

2. I sincerely believe tea and snacks have no place in a meeting; take a break, have the tea and come back. Waiters in the room are a distinctly bad idea. I know Indians show respect by offering food or tea — but do the respectful act before and after the meeting — not distracting a thirty minute meeting with noises like "sugar, one or two?", people moving about etc. This affects productivity.

3. Surface your disagreements. Make your stand clear; after that, commit to your decision. People are passive-aggressive in the US. Indians, being more polite, don't voice disagreements, but don't buy in either. I say, "Speak your mind and then shut up and toe the line."

Sherry Murphree

One thing I distinctly remember we had to work on adjusting was time. The timing of phone conferences became an issue. The expat teams wanted the calls during their office time, which made it difficult for the Indian team. After a while we decided to alternate, so one call was at a convenient time for the expats, and then the next call was at a convenient time for the Indian team. That way inconvenience is shared and all feel respected.

 It's a fact...

A good example is that of a very senior African-American woman, a former senior US Government health official, now working at the Bill and Melinda Gates Foundation, which was interested in offering health assistance to India. On her first visit to India, I discussed the protocol of meetings with very senior Indian officials. I tried to explain that in India she had none of the personal relationships that are so important for doing business or achieving agreements, so, she should focus on building a relationship of trust first. She was taken aback and did not welcome my advice, arguing that she should just be her own congenial self in the same way that she dealt with people elsewhere. Moreover, she thought that she, as a minority, already knew how to deal with non-Western people. In the end it took her longer to break through, as our American directness can slow down progress in Indian meetings, if we don't adjust it to suit Indian protocol.

– David Sloan

Phil Spender

We had to work at making meetings effective; it didn't just happen. Finding a way to allow Indian nationals to participate more easily in meetings was very important. At first they were rather quiet. The process was to give them their voice. Indians speak beautiful English, so if we give them the opportunity to speak and draw them out, by assigning roles, Indian teams can be most forthcoming and productive at meetings.

Our best practices and processes worked so well in India that we went to China to set up the China plant, replicating the Indian model. Meetings there were more complicated, with interpreters needed in China, as I ran meetings in Chinese to get them comfortable.

Shanker Annaswamy

Apart from people from different countries, even teams from India may come from different cultural backgrounds. Hence, it is best to establish a common code or protocol for business meetings, so that we achieve the objective.

Meetings must have an agenda and the same should be conveyed to participants well ahead of time, so that the participants come prepared. As a leader convening the meeting, I always tried to start and end meetings on time. The agenda normally will have time slotted for introductions in the beginning and at the end for closing remarks and summary. There have been occasions in meetings where to encourage broader participation, I would actually announce seemingly simple things like, "Please speak up and everyone will get an opportunity to do so. Please let one person finish and then present your point of view. We will leave the last ten minutes for Q & A, so please take notes and do ask questions in the end."

It's a fact...

When I was working at GE Yokagawa Medical Systems in Tokyo, the Japanese team members arrived early for the meeting, but would not enter the meeting room until the meeting start time. In France, the luncheon business meetings may be longer than what we are used to, but there is no point being restless in that environment. Getting comfortable with the uncomfortable is key to reach middle ground.

– Shanker Annaswamy

Another thing I have noticed in the meetings in India, the teams are reluctant to bring up contentious issues in the meeting and capture them as they are discussed in the minutes of the meeting document. The minutes of the meeting document are generally prepared to reflect a good meeting in most cases. There have been occasions, where I have gone back to the team to amend the minutes to reflect the true discussions in the meeting. The teams need to understand that such meetings are held to bring out tougher issues on the table and solve them cross functionally.

While such an agenda gives a framework, it is also

important to appreciate the cultural diversity, when we operate with different teams.

Zia Mody

If it is an all-Indian meeting, I am conscious of the seniority of the players, of promoter presence, of high level chief executives. Indians expect that there is a certain approach you have to take, when you are dealing with them depending on their positions, and I think there is nothing wrong with that. You can't really say everything in the same bottom line way as you can with Americans. For the Americans, they often come as a group with people in different roles — one could be a business development person, one could be a legal counsel, one could be a compliance person, and so on. You really need to address each one's agenda in that meeting, and not leave out the topic for which that person has flown out all the way to India to see you.

Zia Mody

If it is a new client, we look up what the company is about, make a few internal calls, have some quick discussions within the team that is going to lead the meeting. If it is an existing client, then there is already an agenda when they come to see us. Sometimes the agenda says in the email "Let's meet for coffee" and then, we guess what the client would like to know: the economy, the politics, the way forward, the green shoots, so that they go back with some sense of where India is going. If it is a specific meeting, then, they give a fairly specific agenda, so no time is wasted.

Kirthiga Reddy

One thing that clearly comes up between the US and India is the meeting time zone. My manager used to do his one-on-ones with me on my time zone, and it was interesting, as I had to do these with seven people, but the only one who did it on my time zone was my manager. That sends a message. I do think that this is best practice for leaders — to do meetings in the other person's time zones. It is incredible how many times we Indians think we have to be the one that takes a late night call, whereas, if you just step up and rotate it, six months on my time zone, and six months on your time zone, people empathize. It's hard when you are just setting up, to push back on that one, but it's worth it.

It's a fact...

It is true we have different cultural perspectives. In the early stage, senior people from our India team visiting Tetley had to wait in the Visitors' Lounge before being taken to see the leadership team. They carried the hierarchical cultural baggage of India and it was uncomfortable for them to be made to wait. We had to mentor the senior leadership, showing them how we are all part of one organization, and convince them that we really needed to drop these barriers, with which we were used to operating. It led to an open office concept. My role as Chairman of Tata Global Beverages involved constantly dinning cultural concepts into my teams, apart from business and revenue goals, so that we might diffuse minefields of culture.

– Krishna Kumar

Krishna Kumar

Adjusting to a meeting protocol is about doing what they usually do on the other side. I imbibed the key

Western disciplines when I held meetings in the US, and I did my very best to be absolutely on time, whether it was in New York on Wall Street or elsewhere. I spoke to their values and showed discipline. I find that many expats are sensitive to cultural issues here too, the early stage of dialogue can be a little prickly, but when you cross the barriers, things smoothen out.

Tips from...

Kiran Mazumdar-Shaw

Don't complain too much about the other side. Accept differences. What is most important to being a global citizen and part of a global company is proper systems and processes, an international work ethic, and adapting worldwide best practices.

It's a fact...

When I was running one of my first meetings in America, I expressly stopped the meeting and asked participants what their preference was, to continue the hackathon and finish the topic, or to reconvene. I asked, "It looks like this particular topic could take all of thirty minutes. Do we have agreement that this is important enough that we take those thirty minutes and let another agenda item drop?" The people who had prepared for the last agenda item also were present and getting them to say it was okay worked very well. Getting consensus on this from the majority was important, and my manager congratulated me for this step.

– Kirthiga Reddy

How can I get Indians to speak up more as equals to me?

Ravi Venkatesan

You can spend time in the beginning of meetings to make the Indian more comfortable around you and encourage open dialogue. The fact is, we come from 100+years of colonial rule, and there is a bit of diffidence. We are hierarchical, and a bit subservient. So I urge the American manager to ease people's minds, get people to feel confident and secure around you, by speaking directly to their issues in so many words. "Do I intimidate you? Is my accent hard for you to understand? Shall I do something specific to make you feel more relaxed?" Build a relationship of trust, and break down the diffidence. Then the teams will naturally speak up more and generate great ideas.

Stuart Milne

One thing we did to achieve this purpose was called HSBC Exchange. We run HSBC Exchange meetings without agenda. Everybody can say what they have on their minds. The boss chairs the meeting (but does not lead the discussion), junior and senior staff speak their minds on what they think is broken and needs to get fixed, and we use this way to break down barriers. It seems to reduce the fear of speaking up, as people say less and less the "Why did you say that to Stuart, why didn't you tell me first?" kind of thing.

Why don't Indians lock down meetings in advance instead of going along for last minute ones, based on 'who' called it, unsure of the agenda?

Kiran Mazumdar-Shaw

I find that Indians are actually more accommodating about taking meetings, and I am sorry to say, foreigners are inconsiderate, abruptly stating, "Sorry,

I have something planned." I agree though, that the one key thing for meetings is to go well prepared. I must stress the importance of preparation and encourage people never to just 'show up' at a meeting even if the super boss calls it. In our company, we select people who are well equipped, prepare them for meetings, internally discuss with key people to enrich that preparation, carry out due diligence and do background research, so the time spent is optimized for all concerned. I was in Japan recently and it was different culturally, yet the same internally. When we come into a coffee-cookies room, there is a sense of comfort automatically.

Kirthiga Reddy

This is now changing; although some years ago in India, I had seen meetings simply extend beyond the stipulated time. No one said anything about it, simply allowing the meeting to run to a logical end, as it was for the organization's benefit, capitalizing on the fact that all the senior leaders had gathered around the board room table. But in the US, it is etiquette to start and end meetings on time with all the agenda items covered. Leaving any unfinished topics is seen as poor planning on your part. If the boss calls a meet, the Indian mindset of deference to hierarchy prevents asking too many questions, and they go with the flow.

Many professionals are taking a page out of the global book now and speaking up, asking politely "What do I need to come ready with?"

It's a fact...

Hierarchy existed in meetings and I wore the badge of honour to break it down. It is important to feel the true pulse of the organization at all levels. There was an Assistant Manager I remember, who would say she was torn between two bosses, having to stand up when her Indian boss walked in, calling him Sir, versus just calling the super boss, who was Australian, by his first name and being much more relaxed around him. Modern business is much less formal and part of globalization is attempting to level it out.

– Phil Spender

How can we help Indian team members if they don't ask questions at meetings and later during implementation, we find they didn't understand instructions?

Kirthiga Reddy

In a one room meeting scenario, it's hard to get people to speak up in India. People will leave the meeting without getting their questions answered, thinking they will figure them out later, while it is much easier to get the answers right there. I find it effective, when there is someone who understands that and asks, "What questions do we have that have not been asked, let's put them out now." This helps to overcome the cultural biases.

Tips from...

Global Adjustments

Indians want to respect the managers, so at times, don't ask questions. Americans want to respect the managers so they do ask questions to show they were listening and to not to take up time later on. So the underlying value is respect for both sides. However for Indians, it's a matter of saving face — just in case everyone else has understood, they remain quiet, not wanting to be the only one needing an explanation.

How do we encourage quick stand-up meetings to resolve issues, over the Indian tendency of sitting right next to each other and sending out multiple emails?

Zia Mody

I guess it's about not wanting to be confrontational, somebody internally hesitating to bell the cat. We have become a slight culture of ping pong, and it is a wrong behaviour pattern. When you see it happening, call the people in, have them sit in your room and talk it through in front of everybody. If this is done explicitly a few times, the neighbourhood email syndrome will reduce.

How can today's global citizen develop boldness and self-confidence with cultural sensitivity in a short period of time?

Krishna Kumar

The only way is to make this part of one's conscious learning. Know yourself and your own cultural behaviour first. Then acclimatize yourself with the mores of the other side. And adapt behaviour to bridge the gap consciously. Intellectual corporate people should begin to appreciate the changing world and acknowledge that geography specific is not the norm anymore for business. The important thing is to be able to shed the cultural baggage you carry with you. Tata's acquisition of Tetley Tea was one of the biggest cross-border transactions at the time. Tetley was three times the size of Tata Tea. Our acquisition of Tetley was a clear indication of our attempt to understand the changing world. We realized that India-specific wasn't enough. Though we were market leaders in India, we realized that we had to assimilate a global culture. Synergies were there as well with the two entities.

However, the real challenge was to integrate the company into a global enterprise. We had to merge people from all over the world. Mergers and acquisition need a uniform cultural vision.

One of the first things was to have global conferences. Prague was our venue the first time, when the new company was being formed. (It is now called Tata Global Beverages). We had to sit down together and chart out the goals we hoped to achieve, and think about areas where we needed a new cultural platform. We had this useful exercise lasting two or three days, which I quote now as a best practice. There were other entities like Tata Coffee and Eight O'clock Coffee, a US company, in the mix. We set about creating a virtual organization which still exists. It draws ideas and strategy to maximize synergy and create uniform cultures from senior people from different geographies and from all parts of the company. Combining forces and working toward a common goal, setting aside old ways of doing things independently, and leveraging the strength of cultural diversity, is the best way forward.

Why do Americans seem impatient with the structure and length of our meetings?

Sherry Murphree

We, Americans, place a very high value on speed and efficiency, meetings have become shorter and shorter, and we can both learn from each other; but we need to work out joint understandings.

It's a fact...

I once had a Western manager who didn't have any chairs in his office, and you had to keep your comments short and quick. We didn't even sit down, just said what we needed to say and moved on. That was very efficient on time.

– Sherry Murphree

How can I learn to use humour in an intense business conversation/meeting like Americans do, to diffuse a situation?

Stuart Milne

What I find is that it's more about getting to know the people you are meeting. Use self-deprecatory humour, it breaks down barriers, rigid meetings will become relaxed.

Tips from...

Global Adjustments

Indians are said to be serious by nature. One ranking placed India at #123 among countries that smile, where Denmark was rated #1. But the humour has to be about ourselves, we have to take ourselves lightly and laugh about 'us', not about 'them'. Once, at a meeting, an Indian manager, taking a cue from an American, who was using idioms, said, "Let's work hard to find a solution, and in the evening we can let our hair down — at least what little you have left of it." This reference to the balding American didn't go down well at all.

Why won't American meetings accommodate new discussion topics not on the original agenda?

Stuart Milne

It's a very Anglo-Saxon way of working. I have worked in the US, where there was this disinclination to discuss topics not on an agenda, and I have also worked in France, where it is not like that at all. In fact, in Paris, the French explained it to me like this: "You Anglo-Saxons take one problem and by logical steps you work out that problem, before moving on to the next one. We are French, we love to juggle many problems all at the same time." Explaining this difference upfront may lead to increased acceptance on both sides.

Zia Mody

It's true that Americans want to stick to what's written down; they don't want to deal with the unexpected. But, they will be flexible, if it is explained to them properly. For example, there was this one FMCG client who came to India, with a very short window to clinch a deal. But when the team needed to engage with a topic outside of the agenda — in this case, explain the Indian states, and how a new one had been carved out — some time had to be spent on the political and geographical overview of India, because it linked with the way they would set up their regional presence. This nuancing and flow into the original topic worked well. They were happy to spend some more time on this, although they didn't know we were going to be discussing this when they originally factored time for the meeting.

Before the start of an in-person or virtual meeting, expats engage in small talk. Do I have to do this also, and how do I get good at it?

Kirthiga Reddy

Well, what I can say is, small talk really helped me, but I had to learn to become good at it. I remember one of my direct reports told me, "Kirthiga, one of the things you should think of is you come in, and you are super focused on what you are doing, and then you leave. You may want to spend time to get to know the people you work with." It was an eye-opener for me! This was the time my second child was born. I had to get my job done and be in and be out. It was incredible to me that 'relationship' was what was missing. Things can become much more difficult or easy with work projects, depending on the relationships you develop. In my case, I would go have a cup of coffee, and go out and ask about their family. Just step away from the work situation and connect as human beings, and every single time I have taken the time to just connect, it has become smoother. You need to remain genuinely interested in the other person and able to nurture their likes. One of my colleagues dedicated herself to learning football, because she knew her team was very fond of it. So, take interest in their interests.

Tips from...

Global Adjustments

Kirthiga Reddy is your average Mom. She is no different from other moms whose children are demanding. Her children are not any less insistent on snack food. Her balance of Mom power, instinct to do the right thing and motherly love to do the kind thing are just as much in conflict as in any of us. When, in the midst of an interview, part of a very long day, she gets a call from her babysitter, that Arya would like some chips as they make the dinner go down better, she excuses herself from the interview, and negotiates a substitute — the Indian fried lentil crispies called 'appalam'. She comes back to the interview, is polite about ending it on time, and immediately goes on to the next task on her agenda. It is all about juggling things, being firm and patient.

During meetings, our team feels intimidated by the Americans' style of questioning. How do we get them to soften their approach?

Jukka Lehetela

Indians can talk to the Americans one-on-one to say what the team is feeling. It is the responsibility of the expats to soften their approach, really.. These discussions can provide background information in more detail, so that the expat knows how not to make questions too rough or too fast. Personally, I try to soften my approach with laughter, or I explain why I want to know something. I find that always providing a bigger picture and more information helps smooth a situation. Learning to read body language and slowing down helps too.

How and when should Indian interlocutors correct a Westerner when they make wrong statements about Indian history or culture — or mangle the pronunciation of Indian names or words?

David Sloan

This is often a problem. For example, a number of years ago when former Minister of Finance P Chidambaram visited New York, I arranged an invitation for him to speak at a breakfast meeting in the US Council on Foreign Relations. When the moderator, the Chairman of PepsiCo, introduced the former Minister, he spoke of his good friend 'ChidumBEARam', an unfortunate mispronunciation that caused me, and probably Mr. Chidambaram, to cringe. I have always urged that companies must make sure their expat staff and visitors know the correct pronunciation of Indian words, especially names. When this is not done, I advise just using 'Sir' or 'Madam', to avoid embarrassment. There are also innumerable small business-cultural differences that cause confusion. Very few foreigners, for example, have any idea what a 'Vote of Thanks' is, or how central it is to the Indian business culture in an event or function. Another example is that in a meeting, one should never directly and publicly correct an official; rather, one should take the official aside after the meeting and suggest, say, some improvements for next time. Indians don't usually correct in public, and when they do so, they do so very gently. The American working with India needs to read up on it, or be ready to say he doesn't know much, and that he's open to correction. This makes it easier for the Indian who can take the American aside and guide him. For eg., he can tell him gently that "Are you Hindi and do you speak Hindu?" are not apt questions, explaining that Hindu is the religion and Hindi a language. By adding "I know it's easy to confuse the two", he can make the American feel he's learnt something, rather than that he's made a stupid error.

Why don't expats understand that a head 'wag' doesn't necessarily mean that we Indians agree with an argument or a point?

David Sloan

Yes, American visitors often ask me what the unique Indian head 'wag' means. "I don't get it," they will complain. I have to explain that Indians, like Japanese, dislike saying "no." I explain the complex difference between true intention and the polite gloss, contained in the head 'wag'. It may mean "I am listening to you, but cannot, yet, tell you what I think." So, I advise the visiting American not to draw conclusions, but rather to analyze the situation. And ask for clarity. Or, extending the body language to accessories, the foreigner may ask "Why does this guy have so many rings? He has rings on all of his fingers." I have to explain the meaning in India of auspicious stones and family treasures, and that it is no big thing if a man wears four or five rings.

How do you conduct yourself differently in meetings with government officials/bureaucrats/babus than in meetings with other businesspeople?

David Sloan

I explain to foreign visitors that the lustre of the old ICS (Indian Civil Service) has diminished. Bureaucrats don't make a lot of money, but they have interesting jobs with a lot of power. Much of that power is manifested in the respect an IAS (Indian Administrative Service) officer is accorded. Thus, anyone doing business with the Indian government must understand and not push IAS officers around. They must understand what is possible, and that the IAS officer is the person who can make things happen. The Secretary is important, but he is not the worker bee. The Minister, moreover, may not have much understanding of a particular issue, leaving the issue in the hands of the IAS officer. Another issue is the tendency for Westerners to break protocol by talking to lower level officials or breaking the chain of command. Rather, lower level employees or expats should be delegated to talk with lower level officials.

CHAPTER 3

PERSONNEL MATTERS

"People are the same; it is the habits that are different," said Confucius, the Chinese philosopher. In this chapter, about the hiring and firing of people and the forming of teams, we ask questions about the different habits that perplex managers of multi-cultural teams as they conduct business beyond borders. Some of the behaviour of people seems irrational, till we understand the deeper values that drive them in the family and at the office. Without people, there is no business, so let's take a look at what makes workers join a multi-cultural team and stay motivated, and how to reduce their exits.

Pray it works
Photo: Yngve Andersson, Sweden

What have you found to be the most challenging Human Resource issues in building a bi-cultural team of employees?

Phil Spender

To do recruitment in India, the Westerner has to have an open mind and be willing to initially micromanage more than he is used to back home. We choose raw talent with intelligence and open mindedness; we want people who are willing to learn. There are plenty of them, but they have less experience. Time has to be given to grow them. We can do the teaching, guiding, and developing and terrific results are assured. Some of the Indian nationals, who we hired, are now expats at Ford themselves in the Asia Pacific. You can fill your global team leadership seats from India, if you invest time in the people here.

It's a fact...

The Ford Ikon model wouldn't have been successful, if we hadn't done the Ford Escort in the first place. India was our learning laboratory, we had no recent experience of Indian markets, and had to get the market pulse, understand the terrain, heat, humidity etc. It was the Indian team that met constantly and contributed greatly to getting it right. We got strong Indian input in our success.

– Phil Spender

Ravi Venkatesan

Hiring talent is a less developed eco-system in India, it was only perfected about twenty years ago. The depth of seasoned managers is still pretty thin, so it is, overall, a far greater challenge here. As a leader, you have to do an enormous amount of teaching. Somebody doesn't know how to make a presentation — you can't get irritated. You have to be patient the first time, do some training, and then it's okay to get impatient the second time. Managers don't know how to hold others accountable. The monkey is on their back, so they have to be taught how not to take it on themselves, and learn how to make the system work. Microsoft and Cummins were huge organizations I ran, and they attract great talent, so our challenges were limited, but teaching was still a need.

Americans are more transactional, and are here to just get the job done. They find it odd that people ask personal questions. This is only an innocent interest by Indians — who are by nature interested in you but are not team players. Personal accountability (or the lack of it) is a shortcoming in our culture and we don't take responsibility. Giving excuses is not just an Indian way, it is merely more pronounced here in India.

Also, we in India are very poor listeners. We interrupt. Three people speak at the same time. This is off-putting to Westerners. I have said in my book — *Conquering the Chaos*, "Indians are lone wolves." Our managers are very often competent, but they don't know how to hunt in packs. Collaboration is not a strength in India.

The way to solve this is to try to create a company culture that is different from the national culture. For example, spitting is part of our national culture, but we don't accept it in our company. So it is entirely possible to create a healthy and good work culture in other areas, while still respecting the culture.

Sherry Murphree

There were quite a few things to learn about human relationships particular to India. While interviewing people, we learned that if we were interviewing a single person in an Indian joint family, there was reluctance to relocate due to family obligations. While they may move initially, they would want to return to their home because ties and responsibilities to siblings were prominent in their lives. We adjusted our interviewing techniques and asked about family matters up front, that way we could adjust our HR packages to the family needs of the person.

It's a fact...

We had one company, after they started their first round of meetings, ask us how they could have a successful joint venture outside of the signed document. It turned out there was a daughter of the Indian partner in the picture, a bright girl, important to the father as his successor in the company. The foreign partner had to demonstrate that they agreed with this succession plan of the promoter (father). Consequently the father, who valued this outward display, increased the trust quotient he had with the Western company.

– Zia Mody

Shanker Annaswamy

The successful teams are those who appreciate diversity and welcome different points of view. It is all too easy for both sides, based on their cultural backgrounds, past experiences and what they believe as right and wrong, to judge and form opinions of the other. I have found that teams that have built informal relationships bond well together and help each other in times of need.

With respect to letting employees go, one has to be careful not to cut and paste the same process that works in the western world to India and vice versa. In the USA, while the process of the pink slip is painful and the concerned employee goes through a traumatic period, what helps the process of resettlement is the well-developed eco-system and the business environment. It is a practice that is known to employees and the eco-system provides alternate options to the affected employees. In India, the situation is different. Many develop an emotional attachment; some may harbour an entitlement culture irrespective of performance. So it is very important to establish clearly, quarterly and yearly performance appraisals and communicate candidly. The rules and standards of employee promotion, career progression and separation need to be established, communicated and practiced. This will lessen the pain of separation whenever a situation arises in a company. In many companies in India the employees are provided an opportunity to resign, except in cases related to failure of integrity and malpractice.

Zia Mody

As someone who has facilitated numerous multi-cultural mergers, I feel that the main thing for good team dynamics is the level of engagement each side is willing to provide to the other. Does the foreigner remain feeling the outsider? And if so, for how long? Does the Indian feel insecure or threatened, or that there will be peer comparison? If so, how do you break down those insecurities? I have seen CEOs who are expatriates come to India and be part of the organization for years; they have gone out with their Indian colleagues, watched theatre, broken bread and there is a genuine friendship. So, I guess people from different cultures can actually become good friends on a human level; and if you can get them to do that, then, at least at the workplace there is a sense of co-operation.

Tips from...

Zia Mody

An important factor is making Indians feel that they are valued in the global space of multinational companies. Very often I say, "Why don't you make Indians part of global committees, take them to global conferences, and treat them as valued partners, because trust begets trust. The crux is to make each side feel that they are both of value, then the combination of $1+1 = 4$, happens when they team up. If business is to grow, extracting the value of cross culture is absolutely crucial."

Jukka Lehtela

Hiring expats for India is a particular HR challenge. When Nokia set up business in India, we had to use strict measures to find expats to come to work in the country. They either love India or they hate it, so, choosing the right person is very important! Make sure that you select people who have a positive view about India — they have to be open-minded and a have a very good attitude. On the other hand, when we hire Indian people, we give preference to those who have external world views and have been outside India for a while. That way we found we could create a better succession plan. Find someone with a global mindset, ready for a common culture, so that they can help build a company culture. This was key for us, and I highly recommend it, as there are many 'glocal' Indians available — local and global at the same time — people who can be crucial for the entire team.

Kirthiga Reddy

I have worked at this high bar company, Facebook, where you hire when you find the right person, versus taking a measure of time in which you have to close a position. I have seen cases where you hire after interviewing ten people. Find one person who you make the offer to, versus pondering, "Is that the perfect person for that job?" Make sure that you are not doing a local maximization, but rather, fit the right bar. Otherwise you don't get a seat on the Facebook team.

Tips from...

Zia Mody

One challenge we faced was that Indians are willing to stretch themselves beyond work hours. Conversely, foreigners have a real 'watch the clock' syndrome; every holiday is sacrosanct; they don't entertain calls at night; Christmas means 'No Interruptions.' But of course, they have no issues with scheduling calls during our night times or on our national festival of Diwali. They are very protective of their time, and not so sensitive about ours. Some Westerners have a very strong entitlement mentality. They expect a lot from their company, and talk down about India.

This has to be nipped in the bud. You have to counsel the expat. Explain the global managerial requirements and tell them what the investment is about. Everyone needs to be professional, direct but kind, and not rude.

Krishna Kumar

One challenging human resource issue is mobility. As we are a hotel company, I did not want executives to be in the same place for too long. There needs to be a change of role and location, to bring greater dynamism to the organization. But due to the wife's work, or children's school, it was a challenge to have staff move about. It was something I was firm about. As I wanted a free flow of talent across geographies, it was important to change them from the global entity, and move them from London to Bangalore, where I had to bring talent. Once I had to send a conservative person from Bangalore to the US but, making those moves painless but firm was important for the global success of our organizations. Overlooking cultural limitations of food and dress, people had to be taught to freely move about and contribute overall. It needs planning, and time spent with the employee, to get him/her to be productive in newer locales. People in India don't uproot themselves as easily as in the US, where mobility from one state to another, even coast to coast, is considered an adventure.

Do you have any tips on recruitment that are specific to India?

Stuart Milne

The employer brand being strong in India is key to getting the best people to apply. Many from the IIMs (the premier Indian Institutes of Management) apply to our company, for instance. We have no trouble in hiring, other than the fact that the fifty-fifty gender balance, which we would like, is not there.

When you are talking to people about their career plan, it is very important to know a person's family situation here in India, much more so than in other countries. We, at HSBC, for instance, like to send people overseas, as they learn and come back and contribute better here. But in India, if your recruit is the only son, or the eldest son of a family, it will affect your plans, as he may have to take his parents with him to Hong Kong,

I do encourage expat bosses to spend time outside of the office to know their team and their family situations. For example, I do a dinner twice a month with different teams, either in my home or we go out. Over drinks and food we get to know each other. I go around in circulation and just pick the team I would like to see each month, or it may be a team that has done something special. We try to cover a broad range, not just the revenue generating teams, support functions are included too. Engaging with colleagues outside the office is more important here in India, than, perhaps is the case in the US or the EU.

Informal networking with spouses helps even with my top team. At least twice a year, we all get together for an evening; it's great fun and has helped break down the formality of how we operate in the office. If we have a more informal relationship, difficult things can be done, or said easier.

What is this obsession with job titles that Indians have, compelling HR to think of an improved title each year?

Sherry Murphree

We learned that job titles are extremely important in India. Global job titles that we may use to derive salary systems within Dow might seem degrading in the Indian context, even though the job itself would be fine. For example, 'Associate Engineer' could mean you manage a team, but it was disturbing for an Indian to use this outside of the company, because it didn't convey enough authority. Corporate groups had to agree to external job titles like 'Manager' or 'Director', and would print those titles on personal cards for people to use outside, but inside the company, we maintained the worldwide structure and titles we use throughout the company.

Krishna Kumar

In the Indian cultural context, designation has a prominent role to play in how you are perceived in society, so you do become obsessed with your title. If you are a bachelor, or a single girl, it can even be the deciding factor in receiving the right proposal for a marriage partner. We have mixed up our careers and designation too closely with our personal lives — so these titles affect us. Western companies, like Indian ones, have realized the importance of handing out titles and improvements, not just salary increases each year, as it motivates employees and reduces attrition.

Jukka Lehtela

Indians are hierarchical and Finns and Americans are not. We wanted to have a flat organization, so, we did the Nokia matrix organization — explaining to Indian people that they may have more than one boss to report to. This was a learning they had to imbibe. We spent many hours teaching them this way in the beginning, and then it became an accepted Nokia India way of doing business.

How do you motivate both Indians and Americans?

Zia Mody

Humans are humans and to some extent, they are motivated the same way everywhere. As a senior lawyer, if I feel an executive has done a great job, I can go out of my way to phone him, send him an SMS, or to tell him so personally. This has a lot of value as honest appreciation. But I also send an SMS when I think it was a bad job. I may not say anything in front of the larger group, as there is a need to save face. I don't think Americans are very different in this aspect; they also need to be dealt with this way, although they can handle a little more direct criticism.

Tips from...

Kirthiga Reddy

My belief is when people in India come to you with feedback on a non-performer, you ask, "Have you told that person directly?" You make sure they received it directly. Sometimes it is hard for people to distinguish between a casual conversation on what one could do better, and a serious discussion on the need to improve and how to do it. I have actually gone up to people and said "On a scale of 1 to10, you are at a 2. Please take this seriously." They can then distinguish the seriousness. Be clear, provide structures to fix weakness and leverage strength, but, when that is not happening, let them resign in the Indian context versus giving them the pink slip like they do in the US.

What is the right strategy for reward? If we praise one star performer on an Indian team in public, there are three others in the back sulking.

Sherry Murphree

This is to some extent true in the US too. In India, we tended to reward teams together, but, there is a philosophy promoted by Jack Welch — be honest with people and reward top performers and get rid of your bottom performers. Our salary structures are usually done that way. That is kind of the way of the world. That said, try to recognize the whole team, if possible. Give certificates for the whole team, for example.

Zia Mody

Good lawyering and how to handle people are all equally important parts of my job. While doling out praise, if it is about one group, then, I keep it in the back of my mind that I should say good things about the other people, as well. I may not talk at the same length about everyone, a couple of sound bites will suffice. I do include everybody, keeping in mind that there are different degrees of great stuff. Americans may not do as much sharing of praise, as they are not aware of how it is in India. But, if you explain this to them, they will get the idea. It is the lack of awareness, not the lack of willingness to do things differently, that causes conflict.

Jukka Lehtela

We had a practice in the factory to reward the operators by reach, touching as many people as possible. When they got good production numbers and customer satisfaction numbers, we gave different people a reward each month. Within one year we had rewarded as many people as possible. Something I learned from India, that was a surprise to me, was that people want to get something which they can take home and show their parents, not just to keep for themselves. They want to show off at home, too!

Phil Spender

One good reward was overseas trips which motivate teams in India. Working for a foreign company has very good status in India. Design centers in Europe and Detroit were very exciting, so, this was one way we could encourage new or young talent. Have a performance management system that is openly communicated, and administer it with transparency. People will begin to get comfortable.

At a lower level, also, we rewarded by what we called 'the little ones'. Day in and day out at the factory, the jobs well done, were celebrated with a party, dinners, and recognition. Indian teams like this.

In India, top-down orders seem harsh, but seem to work. How should I give instructions?

Ravi Venkatesan

Treat the other as you want to be treated — this is the golden rule. I am soft spoken, but have had no problem being taken seriously. Be clear and firm, while still being soft spoken and respectful. The Indian who is harsh to his junior is doing the wrong thing. You wouldn't want to work for him, would you? So, give clear instructions without being rude, and get the job done.

Indians don't seem to like to work in positions with clear accountability. How do we get them to change?

Shanker Annaswamy

Sometimes in India, people think their job is important when their scope is wide and covers many areas. In such cases, it is better to clearly lay out the primary goals and the responsibilities where they will have a more influencing role. Explain the 'nice to have' versus 'need to have', so, they can truly achieve the objectives, for which they are being measured.

It's a fact...

Nokia had taken two floors of office space. We asked two teams to clean one floor each. They did the work, but no one cleaned the stairs in between! We had to give very clear and explicit instructions to get Indians to get the job done the way we wanted it done. When I ask people to be accountable, I don't just say "Do this." I ask them to use their own way to get the job done, and show me the results. If they understand the big picture of what they have to achieve, then, they can use their own judgment to get things done, going forward.

– Jukka Lehtela

What is the most important aspect of building a bi-cultural team?

Kiran Mazumdar-Shaw

Groups tend to socialize with each other at work, but rarely do they do the same after work, and this is very important to build bridges. Very few of us realize that we have to socialize after work. It is not about being a teetotaler or vegetarian. Socializing is just being outside work in an informal atmosphere — inviting them for dinner, spending time chatting about interests, connecting at a human level. This is a key ingredient for multi-cultural team building.

>
>
> **It's a fact...**
>
> At this French company I know, which acquired an Indian one, they had regular difficult board meetings as the transition happened. Every quarter, now, after a whole day in the board room, going out to dinner with the board is the norm. Both sides say this breaking of bread together has helped smooth out the roughness of the day in a way nothing else can.
>
> *– Kiran Mazumdar-Shaw*

How does an American boss retain his position when he openly admits to his subordinates that he doesn't know something?

Sherry Murphree

Forty years ago, when I started my career, bosses never said they didn't know something; but now, seeking the knowledge of the whole team is the way to get better results. You have to make Indians understand that you, as the boss, may not have all the answers. You are in the role because of managerial and leadership skills, not necessarily technical skills.

Why are expats given perks so disproportionate to their position and so disparate from mine?

David Sloan

One might explain to the Indian staff that this is a company policy, and practiced worldwide, not just in India. This involves company benefits for employees serving abroad. It is standard company policy to ease the transition to work and life abroad, and not a discrimination against Indian employees. One could, in the right situation, also explain that in the US, there is a concern these days that the wage gap has become too great between senior-working compensation and those at lower levels of organizations, and needs to be re-adjusted.

Stuart Milne

In most global companies, there will always be a certain number of expatriate staff: Indians going overseas and foreigners coming to India. Indeed, this is why many high calibre people are joining multinational companies. Typically, expatriate staff are given certain allowances, such as accommodation and education, to compensate for the fact that they are no longer in their home country. Certainly in HSBC, this is very well understood by our executives. Actually, HSBC India is very much a net exporter of talent to the rest of HSBC, so Indian executives are a beneficiary of this.

What do you think about the practice of hiring NRIs to head up companies in India?

David Sloan

Many companies believe NRIs make the best representatives in India. Many NRIs, however, actually have little understanding of, relations with, or experience in India. They are often out of their depth culturally, or with the Indian subject matter. Indian employees will look at the NRI's community, language, religion, school, etc., which are important determinants of how they view that particular person and of the respect they will show him. Thus, NRIs, who grew up totally overseas or out of touch with India, can actually be a disadvantage for a company, because they don't know how to function in India. It is different, however, for an Indian national, who may have worked for a foreign company in India, later worked abroad, and returns to India.

Stuart Milne

Sometimes there is this view that if a person is of Indian origin, he will lead well in India. Not having lived here, however, and perhaps having lived in

America, he actually doesn't understand things in India at all. Our challenge is more in finding a successor for me and at my level, how do you get the right Indian to be the CEO of HSBC one day? In the past 160 years we have had two Indian CEOs. I would like my successor to be an Indian, who has work experience overseas and understands India, but also has a strong international network and a deep understanding of the HSBC culture and way of doing things.

Zia Mody

I think it needs to be taken case by case. NRIs are coming home to be back with family and intelligent ones can straddle both cultures. But the problem is that everybody thinks you are Indian, and that the NRI thinks like an Indian; but, if you are brought up overseas, then you don't think like an Indian and that's where the clash happens. This is where someone like a *Global Adjustments* has to really drill down and say, "Because you look Indian, people will expect you to behave like this, this, and this. And the dos and don'ts are here — let's soften the abrasive style, let's increase the trust of the team, let's share credit more, so you can succeed in the Indian context."

How can I be a good team member or team lead without losing my Indian culture and style?

Ravi Venkatesan

If you are a good team member or a team lead — you are just universally good, you lose no part of your 'Indianness'. For example, time adaption is good to do whether you are American or Indian. Indians, when asked to come on time for a meeting, may see it as adapting to the American work style, but frankly, it is good overall for any organization to build this into the culture of their work style, isn't it? So, lead your team fairly, don't do the 'them versus us' thing. I find it useless to think this way. There is no 'us' and 'them'.

How can an American expat see beyond his cultural lens, if he isn't even aware he has them on?

Zia Mody

I think for an expat he has to pretty quickly have some trusted advisors in the Indian outfit, as we Indians can be a sophisticated lot, and we can see through the shadows and sub-text easier. Plus, from a continuity point of view, it is the Indian team that has been there and done it, so I think it is especially important for a senior expat to figure out whose inner circle can be tapped for advice. One has to remove cultural blinkers and to collaborate 180 if not 360 degrees.

Why do Indians not have the pink slip policy, but seem to allow resignations instead?

Kirthiga Reddy

I think there is a universal feeling that people wait too long to let go of the wrong person. In India, that seems to be even particularly true. At Facebook, we have a very high bar, so our open culture, real time small bytes of feedback, is our very culture. You never have to wait for performance reviews. We have tools designed to be that way; when you give input you have immediate peer sharing. It doesn't come easy to share here in India. In the US, you can have much more open in-person conversations. I have heard this phrase so often: "Oh, but if we let go of this person, who is going to do their job?" That is a very short term vision. "Something is better than nothing" and "They are helping more than they are hurting," are not reasons to hold on to someone. That's not the bar, the bar is, "Are they really rocking it and making a difference?"

CHAPTER 4

WORKING STYLES

You say, 'potato,' I say, 'potaaato,' goes the song; differing ways of doing things make us believe that our way is the best and anything else must be wrong. This chapter brings into focus some work style differences, which we all face when working bi-culturally, but which can be adapted to, in order to improve efficiency in an organization. Some of these questions have been bandied about in internal discussions, but no one dares to ask the other side as to why they work in a particular way. Our CEOs unravel some of these mysteries and give you insights into the how and why of work styles.

Heave Ho!
Photo: Emmanuel Mancion, France

Indian and American cultures are distinctly different, how have you had to adjust your own management style to lead an inter-cultural workplace?

Sherry Murphree

Living in India was the steepest learning curve I had experienced, since I was in college. Things I said casually as boss were taken verbatim — as fact. For example, if I just made a casual comment, not meant to be a directive or decision, I heard it spread throughout the whole building, because they respected the job I held, and everything I said was the law. Therefore, I had to be very careful about what I said in everyday dealings with people on our staff. After a while, I learned to be more careful, but my Indian colleagues also learned when it was appropriate to be serious and when I was being casual. My management style is fostering a very collaborative environment, while maintaining personal accountability for key business decisions and results. I did not find my philosophy in great conflict while in India, but I did make some small adjustments.

Our Indian leaders and employees expected to be given work and goals. They were less prepared to be asked their opinion on accomplishing those goals. We spent a large amount of time meeting with our groups, explaining the company culture and getting feedback on how best to proceed for a successful organization. Some employees readily jumped into the discussion, but others took their time to get comfortable with the process.

I always take a personal interest in each employee and try to get to know them individually. One of the things I have done, since I first became a manager in the early 1980s, is to set up individual sessions on a frequent basis with all new employees, so I can listen to them. I ask about their family, hobbies, accomplishments and dreams. I also ask for ideas on how I can be a better boss. I sensed that some employees felt uncomfortable with some of these questions. I learned that I had to be more patient and just listen. Over time I was able to gain their trust. And one important thing: I had to be careful that I did not appear to favour those employees that opened up quickly, versus those who were more guarded.

Ravi Venkatesan

In a professional management style focused on tasks, which is the norm in the US, you get a job done, accept accountability, and stay on track. In a family management style focused on relationships, of which we have a large number in India, one manages very differently. You serve the extended family. You expect loyalty and they expect you to look after their family situation. I think there is a pretty strong element of this in family managed businesses outside of India as well, such as a UK company on whose board I serve.

I personally would hate the family style, I operate best in the professional management style, and I put my heart into it. One or the other is not better, however. To succeed in India, you need to be a bit patriarchal, employees expect to feel a bit of love, and if it is completely clinical, you don't go too far.

It's a fact...

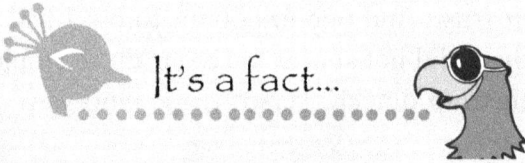

Westerners find the Indian last minute habit frustrating. But there are times when it's amazing too. Our Greenfield Project plant inauguration was on a Monday, and the Indian Governor and our Finnish Prime Minister were coming. Twenty-four hours before the event, there were trailing wires and unfinished trimmings everywhere at our plant in Sriperumbudur near Chennai. I was most worried that I was going to lose my job for hiring an Indian event management company. But overnight, on Sunday, it was like an anthill had opened up, and droves of workers came out, a relay system swung into action, and before my eyes, an air-conditioned tent sprang up, elegantly decorated with amazing fresh flowers, red carpets, the inaugural corner stone and even the logo of NOKIA was put up in jasmine and lotus flowers on stage. There was no way we could have done any better in Finland. I breathed again, and lived to tell the tale, making our company the Number One MNC of India in my tenure.

– Jukka Lehtela

Shanker Annaswamy

I have lived in the Middle East, Japan, and worked for American companies for over two decades. There is no doubt that you have to change your management style and adapt to the local cultural and business practice.

It is not about the language or about simple greetings. During my assignment in Tokyo for GE, the company commissioned a professional agency to coach us on not only culture and history, but also to give us management tips in that work environment. For example, we were told that, generally, the Japanese do not say no to their bosses, but simply exhibit, through body language, that it cannot be done. I found that it was very useful. Similarly the Japanese culture is a formal one and that needs to be practiced in the office and with clients.

In America, it is less formal and quite different how you address an employee or a colleague. You can call them by a first name basis, even if he is a super boss (my boss's boss, for example). However, it is better not to mix the professional and personal side of relationships. I have noticed that weekends, family time and vacation are sacrosanct for Americans. In India, sometimes we tend to go overboard and reach out to colleagues on weekends and vacation times.

Jukka Lehtela

I always find time to build relations and it worked in India, too. I didn't change my management style at all. I was more demanding than an Indian manager. That was just the way it was; and people learned to work with me and my management style. We explained things in much more detail to them, which was the only extra effort we made, to give them a bigger picture and it worked well with this methodology.

David Sloan

As an India specialist for over a quarter of a century, as someone who advises on political developments that affect global companies and investors, I deal mostly with the Indian government, which is a very different world from the private sector. Foreign companies often find working with the government to be very frustrating, although, dealing with the Indian government is clearly important. If a company has a problem in working with a government entity or a ministry — to resolve the problem, my advice is to start at ground level, perhaps seeing the Joint Secretary first to get his advice on what can be done. The company might next seek a meeting at the full Secretary level, but only after demonstrating that the company did its part to resolve the problem. Only then, might the company approach the Minister, who will, in any event, probably not have final say, but rather, have to go to the Prime Minister.

State elections happen periodically and the investor would do well to stay updated with local advice on the outcome of each, as there is no such thing as a pan-India strategy or decision.

Tips from...

David Sloan

It is important to differentiate between the regional/state level and the national/union level, whose responsibilities can be different or may overlap. Overlooking the state can be a big mistake, particularly under Prime Minister Modi, who has clearly indicated that he plans to make states more autonomous, given his own background at the state level.

Phil Spender

Being the country leader is a lonely job. Confiding, getting advice is not easy. And India can be inclusive, but also exclusive. I had to develop more patience than I had, and enhance my listening skills. We are all too confident and love to be heard in the West. Our Indian workforce were lateral thinkers. Using their cultural norms, yet, also thinking outside of the box was important. We ran classes and tutorials at all levels, Indian employees were leaders of the implementation of it. Theoretical learning comes naturally to Indians, so, we adapted that and we leveraged both sides' strengths — Indian and American.

Stuart Milne

The exceptional hierarchy in India is something to be factored in, the seniors expect obedience from juniors, and the juniors don't want to challenge the seniors; so there is an unhealthy respect for hierarchy. It tends to not foster creativity. I say to my teams here, "The way we do things today is not the way to do them tomorrow, there is always a better way to do them."

I do a conference call, we have 5000 staff here across 29 cities, we get 80 telephone lines and about 1500 to 2000 people listen in on those calls, we allow people to submit questions ahead of time. Initially, we used to accept anonymous questions as well as live questions. In the first few calls, I spoke for twenty minutes, and we then asked for questions. There were no live questions and most of the pre-submitted questions were anonymous. But gradually we have gotten to the point where we stop accepting anonymous questions; people are now less inhibited about asking directly. After the calls, we do surveys on whether they liked it, what they would like to see more of, and things like that. And we get good feedback, things like 'the responses are genuine instead of canned company responses.' So getting this open culture to happen in

India takes some work, but it can be successful. This is one thing I want to achieve at the end of my tenure of five years, I want an open culture, with senior staff encouraging junior staff to speak out, and junior staff contributing their ideas.

Why do Americans have this expectation of instant results and unrealistic time frames without taking into account the Indian context?

Shanker Annaswamy

It is not only American leaders who push for aggressive goals, because 'speed' is a true differentiator in the market.

It can happen that leaders, who are expats or from outside India, do not understand the limitations or speed breakers due to the Indian eco-system and set aggressive or unachievable targets or goals. This may result in employee dissatisfaction and demotivation.

In such cases, my recommendation for the leader is to understand and get the facts right about the eco-system from peers. Based on that, set aggressive goals in the form of base target and stretch target with additional incentives. I have seen this work and the team achieve outstanding results.

Why do Indians on my team forget half the things that are said to them, don't take notes –exceed deadlines/delivery schedules? How can I get to do my own job without doing theirs as well?

Kirthiga Reddy

I feel the pain. A lot of it is about communication and setting expectations. The level of exposure that someone graduating from college in the US has is very different from that in India. We invest in making sure that people are trained to know what is expected of them in the workplace, and this is an investment that pays off. It just takes that ongoing coaching. I find it is worthwhile to do it.

Why do Indians, in a customer service or administrative role, irrespective of their position in the pecking order, have to consult someone else before they reply decisively?

Zia Mody

Does it happen that often? Well, maybe because they don't know all the facts. It is a sense of inclusion. If a client comes to me with a question, I will turn to my partner who knows the case. I don't want to give telephonic advice in a vacuum, so, I will say, "What is the issue? Let me check with my partner and get back to you, because I don't know the nuances of this legal issue." In other instances, some may do this because they are not senior enough to make the call. But in our firm, we trust and empower our partners. I am there as their safety net, whenever they need me.

Why don't expats involve us in the bigger picture?

Kirthiga Reddy

I think you earn your way to be involved in the bigger picture, by going to them with your thoughts on where the company should be going. It's asking questions at the right junctures, it's often not what you know, but what you share. It's often the questions you ask that make the difference. I remember when Good Technology got acquired by Motorola, the people at Good Technology said: "What is the strategy? We hired you because you are smart. You tell us." It was a huge learning experience. Have a picture or vision of where the company can go, connect the dots with the organizational goals, but have your own ideas and ask and share. Don't go in there passively and say, "I want to be part of the bigger picture!"

Tips from...

Stuart Milne

For the Indian team, you are part of a global company, there is a company culture and values. If this is not for you, then you should probably be working somewhere else. Behaving in line with corporate values is something that is not negotiable in a multinational organization.

Why don't expats work longer hours, or on weekends even when a project needs it?

Sherry Murphree

Often expat managers have other responsibilities in the office, which make them work late into the night; for example, they may have to call headquarters in the US. So sometimes it is not visible what other responsibilities people have. In America we do follow the philosophy of work hard, and play hard. So, personal and professional time are divided into watertight compartments. But, of course, there are some lazy people who don't work late or hard enough.

How do I balance the work styles of two bosses — one American, one Indian?

Phil Spender

Learn best practices from both of them, as neither is all good or all bad. The organization itself has to take this seriously. Both sides should be open. Subordinates should be able to learn best practices from both sides. The organization should organize itself properly, so people don't have to make these choices about who to follow.

Sherry Murphree

This is a case where mentorship is important. You need someone who can help you navigate this. It is critical that someone has a mentor who is not in their chain of command. For instance, we had a great manager in Mumbai, who was Indian, and was very productive and positive in our management meetings. But we heard that he interacted with his employees in a very different way and treated them poorly. Some of these ways were against our principles, so we ended up working with this person, and he ended up changing his working style and was less direct and bossy with his employees.

Americans are coming to work in India and making money here; let them adjust to our work style. Why should we adjust to theirs?

Stuart Milne

I think this is a reasonable demand. We are coming in, and we have to make concessions. I do encourage the American, or any Westerner, to adapt to India. You cannot act as you would have in New York. I say: be less dogmatic or directive in style, understand individuals and family situations more.

How can I be a good boss in India without letting go of the traits I use as a good boss in America?

Phil Spender

Adjust the pace or volume of what you do, as the organization gets used to you. Then you can step up the pace, and allow the natural direction the organization wants to go. Remain aware. Close your mouth and listen, is what you really have to do.

Why is my expat boss so sceptical when I ask for time off to attend personal extended family functions?

Jukka Lehtela

I have often asked this question in India. If people have a certain number of holidays, why don't they use them for their family functions? I know they believe in good luck days, but not everyone new can understand this and productivity is affected, isn't it, if you have so many days off? We work to stringent deadlines, so we need to limit time off. It is always going to be hard for expats to understand the Indian need for so much time off for extended family affairs.

David Sloan

Americans are much more prone to be workaholics than Indians, and Americans take far fewer vacation days than do Europeans. In the US, it is nose-to-the-grindstone while working, with family often taking second place. This work-life balance is very different, even reversed, in India, where the family unit is very tight and often takes precedence over work. Expats need to understand this different value system.

How do Indian business executives overcome the cumbersome Indian government bureaucracy? Is there a preferred method for cutting through the red tape that makes it easier to do business?

Zia Mody

Over the years, my respect for the bureaucrat has grown steadily. I think he or she is immensely intelligent, by and large, has a superb sense of nuancing, understands what policy is, and understands what politics are. They have a clear sense of the achievable and not so achievable. Before a foreigner walks into that large old fashioned office, first, he or she has to a prepare themselves for this sort of environment. Second, the bureaucrat is a powerful man, so, you have to give him or her respect. Thirdly, when you are messaging as a foreigner, you should be very careful not to talk down to the bureaucrat, because they have, very understandably, a great sense of national pride. They are there, in large part, to serve their country, and if a foreigner is telling them what a horrible experience he has had, or what a bad set of regulations exist, it won't go over well. He has to put it elegantly, temper the remarks with good experiences, and come across as balanced. People who have enough intelligence to put across the points that are achievable, succeed. I know of the delays, which ensued when one investor told an

IAS officer "Give me a clearance in two days, because I am the biggest Fortune 500 company, and we are now in India." Nothing happened! We had to explain to him the eco-system in which he had to work. And then a conversation with the American led the IAS officer to become most engaging. He was curious, and like other intelligent people in his category, wanted to know what is happening out there. He built trust with the credible conversation.

Tips from...

Kirthiga Reddy

I truly believe that in ten years from now there is going to be a sea change in corporate culture and the seeds of it are being sown in companies that are leading from the front today. A Global culture is the only style there is going to be.

Expats are here for the short-term. How do they expect us to believe their actions are for the long-term good?

Phil Spender

There are no guarantees that all are looking at the long term, of course. Individuals are different. They are found out in the end, and don't make it. On the other hand, I have had thirty-five years with Ford and many that I worked with were like me. As an expat I learned the game, and in both of the two expansion markets, India and China, it was about creating a foundation for a good long-term business. Dealers were investing, so you had to have a long-term view. Planning for the new models was not good enough, back then, but is great now with the one Ford strategy. We were always working on getting the right balance of fulfilling customer needs for a long time.

CHAPTER 5

TEAM DYNAMICS

No man or woman is an island, and that is why we need teams to get this global village ticking in unison. This chapter addresses those questions raised over the years pertaining to collaborative work that is needed on both sides. Ideally, we would all like to do business with people who are like us. But in the present globalized world, our Indian or American business partners are unlikely to be exactly like us. It is a question of understanding idiosyncrasies and adapting to them so that together everyone achieves more. In this chapter, CEOs share their thoughts on how to hold onto our individuality and yet amalgamate differences to get the best team dynamics in the work place.

T*ogether, **E****veryone **A****chieves **M****ore compresses appropriately, to the acronym TEAM!*

Working Together
Photo: Paul Fejer, UK

What are the most important changes you recommend to educate employees to think and act globally?

Sherry Murphree

I must acknowledge here that inter-cultural workshops and training on both sides helped us spend time to make the teams more globally comfortable. We were also very generous on the time we spent ramping up; we took the time to educate the Indian teams on our work processes, which then helped productivity later on. We taught on the job — for instance, things like how to deal with the US. Embassy when applying for a visa. We tried not to rush, but explained our goals and expectations. We discussed what clothes to wear in the US. We didn't give employees a big stipend for warm clothes, because it was not that cold in Houston, Texas. But, we told them sandals were not appropriate to wear to work, for example. Video conferences helped to get them ready for a global mindset. We built them into our induction process.

We sent several people back to Houston or Germany and had them take sessions on our management style. I personally made fourteen trips back to the US in my first year in India, to provide training for our Western staff there on Indian work style. My goal was a commitment to equal organization and learning on both sides. We also had top-end buy in and superb support from headquarters to build this centre in India. Everybody from headquarters wanted to come and see everything. If we detected arrogance or a bad attitude on either side, or if they were acting uncooperatively, we corrected people. We called them on it, and took the time to get it respectful and right.

Taking into account seemingly minor details is important to get teams comfortable and hit the ground running. We found that driving in India was completely different from driving in the West, so, we set up appropriate transportation for our teams on both sides.

Zia Mody

Global mindsets depend on the leadership. If the leaders have a more global vision and an understanding that customers and personnel can be sourced from anywhere today, then this message filters down to the tier 2, 3 and 4 of the organization. Unfortunately, not many Indians have this global vision fine-tuned yet. For an expat, he is already seeing things globally, as he has come to India. I think the Indian CEO will be quite different in ten years. Indian promoters are already asking for a global mandate for hiring senior executives.

It's a fact...

The young startup entrepreneur is not afraid of technology and also has the perkiness to see himself as equal to others in the global village. New internet companies are springing up and leap frogging whereas older Indian traditional companies are still thinking if they should change. *If it ain't broke, why fix it* is the old attitude. *What's new and happening* is the millennial approach. India's internet era has come of age and that's why the world is taking it seriously, The founders of Amazon, Facebook and Google all came to India in the same week for in-person meetings and conversations with Prime Minister Narendra Modi.

– A Global Adjustments Insight

Jukka Lehtela

We tried to get people to visit sites outside of India — China or other places, so that they could see something else and learn from visits. They learned from each other. As much as forty per cent of my time was spent with visitors in the beginning and in teaching my team. "We are not alone here," was the message I shared. Other global locations have succeeded bi-culturally and we can learn from each of them, was something I conveyed all the time.

It's a fact...

When an American technical expert was sent over to an Indian IT company, his perching on the desks of his Indian teammates, swinging a leg and chewing gum while asking for an update on day one was not well received. Indians on the team were looking up to him to guide them, and needed to see him be more formal in order to respect him. His Indian manager took him aside and explained this. And John went back to his hotel with supposed 'jetlag' and returned the next day with a formal demeanour, to be accepted instantly by a very motivated team.

– A Global Adjustments Story

How did you hire and mentor people?

Ravi Venkatesan

I have worked only in a large global company as a manager. A huge challenge is getting people to put aside the narrow agenda of their own departments, and think of the well-being of the whole company on both sides. The American manager will think only of what he is measured on. Seeing the big picture is only possible through exposure. If people are rotated into different departments, locations, and different countries, they get a bigger perspective. So it is important to broaden the horizons of the people on your team.

For Indians, the calibre of people is important and adaptability varies depending on this calibre. Accepting a lower calibre individual lessens the ability to take on more responsibility. It will be harder to learn new skills. This is quite disappointing; many companies are forced to recruit mediocre people as the demand is large.

I had far less of an issue because Microsoft was Microsoft. And we got the *crème-de-la-crème*. I had to be a lot more selective in hiring. And once hired, we mentored employees on the direct communication style, which is a hallmark of Microsoft.

It's a fact...

I have started something I call the 'CEO's XV', which has the objective to engage a wider group of our senior managers in firm-wide decisions. A different group of fifteen colleagues join me each time to discuss and make recommendations on a specific problem facing our business. Some of the fifteen will then make a presentation to the following Executive Committee meeting, which will ratify the recommendations. This helps the top team tap into more ideas, and really engages the next level of management in real issues, which need solutions.

– Stuart Milne

How is respect best overtly displayed to my Indian team, without compromising my tight schedule for delivery?

Shanker Annaswamy

The most important thing you can do is share the bigger picture and rationale with your team. We were once building a green field factory in Bangalore, and we wanted to do it in 12-15 months. This was needed to go ahead of the strong competition and gain the first mover advantage. We explained the entire thing to our team, and we ended up completing it in nine months. The teams worked longer hours and they were delighted to be part of a winning team. So, when we ask for something to be done within a tight schedule, chances are they will bring up problems related to roadblocks, or you will have to help them identify likely roadblocks by proactively asking about them. When you enable them with the necessary winning tools, by helping to remove the blockages, you can help the team to achieve the task at hand. That's how you show respect for their challenges and still operate within your tight time frames.

As an American who leads an Indian team, how should I balance my casual, familiar style with maintaining decorum?

Zia Mody

Coming across as formal and efficient is important and you have to work on that as a Westerner. You can't be too casual. You've got to be mindful of the situation. Being boyish and cool and hip doesn't work well in the beginning. You can become friends later on, but at the start, Indians do expect some sense of formality.

As an Indian company working with a Western team, how do we work as equals? There seem to be some power struggles.

Kiran Mazumdar-Shaw

I think we live in a time where the old way of a Westerner thinking of an Easterner as inferior has to go. We simply have to operate on a level playing field. I recently read a newspaper article that expats feel threatened in Bangalore, as auto drivers are telling them to go back to their own country. As a student in Australia, I have also faced racist remarks. People accepting that times have changed is the only way forward. For instance, I bought a German company and as the new owner, they accepted me when I visited and things were cordial. But I know when my team visits to audit, they get treated badly. This patronizing attitude that the West has toward India is something we are all sensitive about, and we can't allow this attitude to affect us. It has to start with us not feeling inferior. The balance is shifting, so please let's operate from a position of strength. As an Indian you have the power and knowledge. We shouldn't reproach ourselves, and we shouldn't become aggressive either. Half the problem is in our minds. Take pride in yourself and in the work you deliver. Adopt the best work ethics, and bring a high degree of professionalism to your communication. You will feel empowered and you can let your self-confidence speak for itself.

Why do Americans make such harsh judgments, branding us as 'liars' if a deadline we had hoped to meet doesn't happen?

Sherry Murphree

It is not right to call anyone names; I would have been upset if I had heard this said. You have to keep it healthy when this occurs. We had a project, which we were handling in Kuwait from India, a wind blew a ship far out into the ocean and a timeline was not met, but you can't be prepared for this sort of thing, for example. At other times, it is possible deadlines are not being met in routine projects, the India team simply needs to proactively alert the US team and over-communicate. In fact it is good to under-promise and over-deliver. Americans see the world as black or white, the grey area, that India has, is not visible to us. So it is time to meet in the middle.

When we feel insulted by something an American colleague or client does or does not do, how should we deal with it?

Kiran Mazumdar-Shaw

Communicate what's in your mind and in your heart,

put your emotions into clear, confident words. One of my friends told me the other day that her team member was ready to resign because a Westerner said, "You have to lick their boots, because they are the clients." What was important was coaching her to not just feel bad and give up, but to speak up for herself. She went back and said to the Westerner, who had used this language, "I don't appreciate being talked to in this tone and urge you to follow Indian language protocol." The Westerner understood, apologized and has toned down since. His old habit does surface from time to time, he's not completely changed, of course, but she regularly gives feedback now, if he crosses the line. She too has learned to not be over sensitive. But if she had not spoken up about how she felt, the importance of it may not have dawned on the Westerner, who was using a Western colloquialism. Her leaving the job sulkily would have gone unnoticed. So in a global world, where different backgrounds are coming into the foreground, it is crucial to address offensive behavior upfront and iron out differences one-on-one, so that the rest of the time can be spent on doing core business.

Stuart Milne

Every situation is different and perceptions count for a lot. A woman came to me the other day and asked for an hour of my time to ask for advice. She reports to someone who reports to me. The reporting manager did not mind and had, in fact encouraged her to come speak to me after she told him what she intended to do. I would have told her reporting manager that I was chatting with her, if she hadn't done so. It's good not to break the chain of command in India; it builds trust here more than in other less hierarchical cultures. Working for a supportive manager certainly helps. It also helps to have a mentor outside of one's immediate business to act as a sounding board.

Why do Westerners break work hierarchy and speak directly to my reports, undermining my authority?

Phil Spender

It's never about undermining. India is very comfortable with hierarchy — with your strong British past. This can be challenging for us Australians or Americans. It is always up to the leader in our culture, so many foreign expats feel they need to be accessible to the people. They have to feel the pulse, so that the middle management doesn't perfume the message. If an expat leader reaches out to a reportee, it is more about creating a participative team style which the manufacturing industry needs, not about insulting the reporting manager. Have a frank discussion about how you feel on both sides. If it comes up, have a one-on-one dialogue and be prepared to understand the other's mindset.

What is the best way to get an Indian team to work on a project with a sustained team outcome in mind, and not just creating something on their own?

Phil Spender

India is not alone in people wanting to go off and do their own thing. To prevent that, the organization has to have aligned its goals with what it's trying to do. Define roles and responsibility. Keep documenting the process and coaching the team to sustain the work. A good philosophy is 'Do what you document and document what you do'. Systemize it and teach it, so that it can be replicated. In our Chennai plant, we had many global best practices with minor automation. All of that learning they have applied to the new plant two decades later in the North. So the manager's job is to set global standards and encourage teams to see the long-term goals. I used to say to our team, "At Ford India, we are trying to build a business that will be here in a 100 years' time and will be regarded as a leader in a whole range of ways." I am proud to see that the Ford Eco sport model, sold here in Australia, where I now live, has been manufactured in our first plant in Chennai in South India.

CHAPTER 6

WOMEN ON BOARD

'Men and women are like two feet, we need both to advance' — goes a saying. Keep this in mind at the workplace. The questions that need answering are about building an inclusive mindset and ensuring that women on both sides feel valued, so they can truly contribute to the bottom line of US-India trade. Like all Indian paradoxes, we have the contrasting situations of women establishing themselves in high professional positions, but still having voices that are only just beginning to be heard at many workplaces. American women, who are used to politically correct behaviour, are confused, as they are judged by a different set of standards while operating in India. This chapter answers some key questions on diversity and gender intelligence. Our CEOs speak of change, which must work at all levels of the company, for gender equity to be taken seriously.

Rowing Ashore with Diversity
Photo: Basia Kruzewska, USA

Are there differences in how you create gender equity in the workplace in India, versus in the West?

Sherry Murphree

Dow has high goals to hire women. Interestingly, we had outstanding applicants in India, which is often not so in the US and even less so in Europe. India leads in technologically prepared women, because of the excellent education system. So we hired many highly qualified women. Also, the exchange of Indian and expat women really created a change in the company — the Indian women were great ambassadors for equity. However, we had to hold an event to showcase ourselves as a company that is a women-friendly workplace and truly values them. We converted quite a few women from that event into employees, who are with us climbing the corporate ladder even today at Dow India.

We invited women from leading engineering colleges and those that recruiting firms recommended, and we found candidates who joined us and still are successful in India.

It's a fact...

There is attrition of women at higher levels. We held focus groups to make men more sensitive. One story I have is that groups of men would schedule many meetings at 7 p.m., and women would have to leave at 6 p.m. to do housework and help with children's homework, and therefore could not participate, or did so unwillingly. So, we radically shut off the electricity at 7 p.m., so they couldn't hold a meeting after 6 p.m.! This made it not just a women-friendly place, but a people-friendly place to work; after all, who wants to start a meeting at 7 p.m. and end at 9 p.m. anyway?

– Ravi Venkatesan

Ravi Venkatesan

When I began working in the 90s, there weren't even women's rest rooms in factories, so creating gender equity was really still at a nascent stage in India, though it was a growing need. I found it important to create role models. Women are more comfortable when there are senior women in the management. They want people who understand their issues. I had more than two women on my management teams at Microsoft and Cummins. We measured people based on their company- or department-diversity. We had a metric to measure this, and expected the HR departments to present women candidates as well as men. CVs from men alone were never good enough — we made this mandatory.

By the time I left Microsoft, we had moved from eight per cent to fourteen per cent gender equity, which was an improvement, but not good enough.[1]

To bring about a women-friendly ambience, we even had to do sessions on the language people used — lewd jokes, even foul language was not acceptable. We had to educate managers that late night partying and drinking to generate team spirit, where women were left out, did not work. We urged them to plan team-building events in a way that was convenient to all employees.

---

1   This means that they had fourteen per cent women in the workforce. It was eight per cent when he started.

Shanker Annaswamy

I had the opportunity to work on this very important initiative, both at GE and at IBM. Compared to the west, we needed to work on many fronts to make an impact through this initiative. In GE it was building the 'GE Women Network' and at IBM India it was called the 'India Women Leadership Council'. We realized that the talent pool needed to be consciously built, and progression within the company needed to be monitored closely, and the need for mentorship was critical. There were many challenges — women dropping off after marriage citing personal reasons, need for flexible work environment, and so on. We launched a well thought out 'Get Women Back to Work' programme to encourage them to rejoin IBM. We organized annual events on this agenda and brought successful women from diverse fields to speak and share their personal success stories. We created opportunities for women leaders to network and learn from each other. Often times, their managers were men. We encouraged them to listen to their women colleagues, coach and mentor them. We even held a 'Recruit Only Women Drive' to bring in additional talent from outside.

Needless to say their personal growth was based on performance, but these initiatives created a special platform for women to learn, network, and grow.

It's a fact...

One of our most promising employees, a woman who ended up heading a business unit for intercultural leadership training for three geographies, was not really qualified for the department she was joining. She had life experience in that field, however, having moved and relocated to five countries with her young family. And each time she had bloomed wherever she was posted. Giving her a chance was low risk as her passion showed. Sending her to crash courses and overseas immersion programmes was all it took for her to absorb the best learnings. And today, she performs with panache, putting to shame our competitors with PhDs. And she does it while being a member of the sandwich generation — with elder care responsibilities on the one side, and young adult children on the other.

– A Global Adjustments Story

Phil Spender

In India, there are societal norms that lower women representation, but we have had a few, though not enough, influential senior women leaders. We listened to them. We had them tell us how to attract others. China was better than India in gender equity and Japan was worse, but India is a place, where if we nurture women to grow them into senior roles, the numbers will increase.

It's a fact...

At the shop floor level, factory workers wore saris and didn't want to wear pants, as it was not in their cultural comfort zone. For Ford, safety was a high priority, containing loose clothing for safety reasons was needed. For the Indian women workers, wearing six yards of cloth wrapped around as a sari was dangerous. We expect people to wear safety jackets over their overalls, or pants in the US, so their personal safety is assured, and also, buttons and things can't damage the cars. Finally in India, we ended up making much longer safety jackets which would be worn tight fitting over women's saris, and thankfully, we had no accidents. To be sensitive to culture, yet keep safe, we formed a work council which would discuss and come to a middle ground. Workforce and management communicated consciously through this forum to make the workplace safe and successful.

– Phil Spender

David Sloan

Gender does affect US business calculations about doing business in India, especially in northern India in light of the recent issues with crimes against women.

In certain sectors, Indian women are treated equally,

notably the banking sector. Many banks in India are run by women. The State Bank of India and HSBC are/were headed by women. So, it is possible for women to reach the highest ranks of Indian companies and it is becoming less unusual to see women lead. Banking, however, is something of an anomaly, as most Indian family conglomerates continue to be very male dominated.

At senior executive levels, women do not have many problems; the problems are at the lower levels. This reflects the attitudes among India's working poor, especially in the north, where women are not treated equally. On the other hand, there is still a big problem finding qualified women to serve as independent directors in Indian companies. Under the new regulations from the SEBI (Securities and Exchange Board of India), fifty per cent of a company's directors must be independent, (i.e., not family). While there is no 'reservation' for women, there is a big push to include women among this fifty per cent. But it is hard to fill these positions with women, if they are unqualified.

Tips from...

Global Adjustments

An Indian Vice-President of a leading corporation once told us that while she didn't mind being hugged or getting a peck on the cheek from Western male colleagues or well-known clients, as she knew it was only done to show friendly warmth, if she felt that an Indian watching might misunderstand, she would quickly take the lead and extend her hand, so that the other person knows that all she wants to do is to shake hands. This on-off protocol might be confusing, but a part of the cultural chameleon role that is often thrust on Indian women in business.

Jukka Lehtela

Nokia was keen to have women in all teams; mixed ages was crucial too. The Nokia concept is diversity. Here in India, too, we tried to get as close as possible to that diversity. If I had fewer female applicants, then, we shortlisted more females at the next interview, provided, of course, they were skilled, which they totally were.

It's a fact...

At Facebook India, we are very fortunate to have a pretty even spread of men and women, and what is even more heartening is that it holds true up and down the chain of management. Fostering this is in the very nerve center of how we do things at Facebook. Sheryl Sandberg, our COO, speaks a lot about 'leaning in' and about 'don't leave before you leave', encouraging women to have a long term career vision. We have had women who have joined us while they were expecting a baby. These are women, who are really good at what they do. They know that we welcome them with open arms. That gives them the courage to do wonderful things along with their motherhood. We give them flexi-time, and work from home options. We have had women who come back after they have had children, after a break, and they will come in at a different level, because they don't have the experience. They soon raise the bar for themselves and grow amazingly. When we were told we should have security escorts for women, who came early or went home late, we just decided to extend that facility to both men and women. Maybe there is a man, who is also not from the city, so, men and women are both included in our way of thinking in everything we do at Facebook.

– Kirthiga Reddy

Stuart Milne

In the bank we run a lot of programmes to bring women out — twenty-five per cent of senior positions for women is the global HSBC initiative. In Asia, we are already at fifty per cent, if you exclude Japan, Korea and India. These three nations are right at the bottom in terms of gender diversity, whereas countries with a strong Chinese culture — China, Hong Kong, Taiwan, Indonesia, Malaysia and Singapore — have always had a very strong representation of women at the senior levels in banking.

One particular programme we run is called 'Ascend', which we put together in India to improve gender diversity. We take a group of high potential women, who are just below the level of senior management, and give them different kinds of input over a twelve-month period. The idea is to give them more confidence. We find that we advertise for a senior level position and women won't apply, because they only have, say, five of the seven criteria needed for the job, while men will apply, even if they only have one or two of the criteria. One of the things is to help women understand that it is okay to be turned down, but they must come forward for the opportunity, and take a bit of a risk. Our Executive Committee has a strong buy-in into this diversity agenda, and will always attend all the networking events for the women's groups and engage with them. Each of those women on the program has a mentor, who is a member of the Executive Committee. Cross-pollinating thoughts from someone, who is not from your area, is key.

Don't you think men make better mentors for women?

Stuart Milne

I think you may be right. I have heard senior women express the view that they made it on their own, so, why do others need all this extra support. We need to take the capable women and teach them that it's okay to step outside of their comfort zone, and promote yourself a little. We need to show them how to be ambitious without being perceived as being too aggressive.

Tips from...

Global Adjustments

The mistake that corporations make is assigning only women as mentors to women, and what happens is they usually end up men–bashing, while a man is more likely to see just the facts and helps clarity emerge. Women empathize with each other on the same things while men simply see data and facts, and set aside emotion. This makes the man a good practical mentor to a woman as he comes with opposite view points to strengthen her, without competing in any way. Having a man and a woman as mentors to a woman would be a winning partnership.

I can't find enough CVs to fill the diversity agenda of our organization. How can I attract more women to come work for us?

Kiran Mazumdar-Shaw

I think word of mouth helps in this case. It is a Catch-22 situation I suppose, if there are more women in an organization, it means it will attract more women. Creating an environment for women to feel safe and valued, and advertising this advantage is key. I know in Dr. Devi Shetty's hospital in Bangalore, for instance, all the security guards are women. This is an innovative way to fill the diversity agenda. In an organization run by a woman, it is easier to attract women. In our case we have twenty-five per cent women.

Why do Indian men seem to stare at a Western woman, yet avoid eye contact when addressing one at a meeting?

Zia Mody

It is happening less and less, but Western women may still be a bit of a novelty. Less exposed Indians may seem to stare a bit more rudely than others. It is best to not have eye contact during negotiations or a meeting — if you are trying to prove a point and you don't want to appear confrontational. Indians do avert their gaze. It is actually respectful in our culture to avert our gaze.

How do we prevent attrition when women get married?

Kiran Mazumdar-Shaw

I think there are two kinds of women. The ones who are career minded and others who resign themselves to their fate. It is hard to change them. They have to want to be different and self-motivation is the only way. You can't really mentor women, unless they want to be mentored. They have to raise themselves by the power of their own will.

Tips from...

Kirthiga Reddy

Kirthiga, how do you manage 100 million Facebook users and two daughters?

I believe in the power of AND versus the irony of OR. When Arya was born, I was in a full-time job and had to travel to meet clients, I had nursed Ashana for a full year, and it was very important for me that I did it for Arya, as well. So this is the time everyone speaks of, when you have to make a choice of profession over motherhood, and compromise on some things. I actually travelled with Arya for the first year, there was a lot that I delegated, but for critical events, when I felt I had to personally be there, I actually travelled with my daughter, and the universe simply co-operated with me. Once you decide to do something, nature conspires to make things happen. In one place, one of my colleague's wife had a daycare center, so she took care of the baby. It wasn't easy, but we always figured out a way.

Another example is volunteering. I have always had, since my schooldays, a community/social side to me. Before I had Arya, I used to volunteer at Stanford Children's hospital every Thursday. When she was born, I couldn't commit to a regular schedule. Someone introduced me to Hands-on Bay Area, which is meant for professionals who can't commit to volunteer for regular times. They work with three hundred odd organizations, and you can sign up on the go. So Ashana, Arya, and I went to soup kitchens. Two hours here and there. We planted saplings. This is what the girls remember. So, here's to the power of AND!

As an American woman, I feel insulted that people automatically expect my husband to be the professional and completely ignore me. How should I handle this?

Zia Mody

I understand this, but that is still unfortunately a part

of life. When I went to a conference in New York, when I was working with my partner, they thought I was his secretary! There is still stereotyping. You just have to stand up and your sound bites have to make complete sense. That's when you are going to be taken seriously, You just have to work harder to be taken seriously.

It's a fact...

Recently, we asked HR to reach out to a young woman, who had left our organization six months ago to get married. She is a traditional Muslim and a bright spark, who contributed hugely to our mobility division. She toed the line for 6 months in her conventional family, and then she was in limbo in her new life. After two rounds of conversation and seeing role model women in our leadership, she is back on board now working, picking up right where she left off and adding more to her plate than before. The organization has to keep track of women that off ramp, stay in touch with them in India, sense their pulse, and gently nudge them back on ramp to fit in, showing them an interesting career path. This is where relationships matter, over tasks, in the culture.

– A Global Adjustments Story

As an Indian male, what are the do's and don'ts while working with single American women?

Sherry Murphree

All women want to be treated as professionals, and be given respect for their knowledge. Some of us carry this burden for others, where women were not expected to be high up in their careers. Some pointers: don't get too personal; don't ask questions about their family and personal lives. Wait for them to share. After they do, speak up, and share your own story, as well.

Do you handle performance appraisals for men and women exactly alike?

Stuart Milne

It is exactly the same for men or women.

Actually, in HSBC, we have reduced our rating scale from a five point scale to a four point scale and we have also moved to rating only once a year rather than twice. In the middle of the year, we simply say if the person is 'on track' or 'off track'. The result is that people focus more on the development discussion and less on what number on a scale they are.

CHAPTER 7

NEGOTIATING THE DEAL

Strengthening your own position, while negotiating, is the best technique, world over. But India has its own best practices and Indians are known to be very masterful in driving hard bargains from times immemorial. The questions in this section are about both sides seeking to get a good deal for themselves, without making the other side feel like it's losing out. CEOs who participated in this section have illustrated some of the cultural differences in bi-cultural negotiating and provided practical takeaways to achieve win-win solutions, while still negotiating for the long-term.

Give a long rope
Photo: Emma Horne, UK

What are the key ingredients to negotiating a satisfactory deal between America and India?

Stuart Milne

Don't take 'No' for an answer. Don't worry about pushing. When you want something from an Indian customer, you can ask again and again. I went to ask a business owner to give us an equity mandate recently. We were not there in the list of banks, we got a lot of push back, but we kept saying "This is why you need to have us there, even if you have others." In some other countries it might be seen as too pushy, in India it gets the right result in the right way. Be forceful in giving your point of view but still stay polite.

It's a fact...

Self-deprecating humour works well in lightening inter-cultural tension. While negotiating a merger with a Dutch team, a stalemate was reached and there was palpable tension in the boardroom. That was when a member of the Indian team stood up, stretched himself, and suggested, "Can we think of splitting the difference, like we Indians do when we go to a restaurant, and split the price by two?" Everyone laughed, and ultimately, this was exactly the winning formula that was adopted. On the other hand, if he had said, "Shall we go Dutch?" it wouldn't have been so well received, as it is an insensitive innuendo about that nation's attitude to money.

– A Global Adjustments Story

Phil Spender

In negotiations, it is important to be realistic about objectives — honest and open — so that no one side feels disadvantaged. Trust is strengthened by putting both needs on the table.

We were desperately trying to make engines in India to improve our cost base. One day, the MD of Hindustan Motors came in, and we had a discussion.

We said we needed an engine, but couldn't afford it. He said, "I have an engine plant, but can't fully utilize it. So, we are prepared to absorb the fixed cost of the plant, which is in the Rajasthan desert, to give you the utilization of it to get engines at affordable costs." Ford paid for all the unique investment and variable costs. This was one of the best negotiations between an Indian and an American company ever, and led to a sustained and scalable advantage for both sides.

Sherry Murphree

Number 1: Don't try to put unrealistic timeframes on how long it will take to do these deals. The Indian sense of time for building relationships has to be taken into account. We also need to explain in depth why we do things the way we do, and why the timing is crucial for our productivity.

Number 2: Be sure you explain the expectation in this relationship and talk about how you will do business together, and in difficult times how you will proceed. The 'divorce' often can be avoided, if expectations are clearly stated in the beginning.

A major part of our work in India was to establish a building to house hundreds of employees. Our company has facilities all around the world, so we were very aware of the environment we wanted to establish. We spent the first few weeks talking to various facility owners, researching the legal and governmental requirements, and shaping our vision for the facility. We also spoke to other local companies, who had experienced similar building projects. Here are a few things I learned along the way:

- An incredible amount of time had to be spent in building a relationship. We were accustomed to checking the background, financial stability and resources for potential partners.
- This time, we also spent time just getting to know the partners and setting expectations on working together. Our partner requested that we hold a ceremony to bless that building before beginning the construction. It was clearly the right step in establishing the relationship.

Ravi Venkatesan

Indians are naturally a negotiating culture, without knowing anything about prices. As soon as we hear a quoted price for, say, a vegetable in a market, we will say that it costs too much. That's our nature.

On the other hand, Americans are very legalistic, they will bring in a lawyer and negotiate every word and add exit options first, even before any entry is made. This makes the relationship a bit difficult and seemingly heartless, at first, for the Indian side.

For the American, a contract is a contract. Indians

expect that circumstances will change, so it can't be such a rigid agreement. Our external environment is so dynamically full of change.

So the bottom line is, try to understand the other's point of view and cultural bias, and develop trust, so you can meet somewhere in the middle.

We Indians must be less penny-wise. Two rupees isn't worth endless negotiation. What will that cost in terms of goodwill? Indians are very value-conscious and price-sensitive. If you offer a little bit more of something for free, it makes a huge difference here in India.

Shanker Annaswamy

Early in my career working for Philips Medical Systems, I had an opportunity to visit Orange county in US and negotiate a technology transfer with another sister company of Philips. This was to manufacture an ultrasound scanner out of the Pimpri facility in India. Although I was an executive at the middle management level, I was sent alone to present the opportunity and convince the company to agree to a technology transfer. It was a successful visit and the project was launched from the Pimpri facility. If I have to give three reasons for this, I would summarize them as follows:

- Presentation of facts based on data and good analysis of the market opportunity.

- The benefit to the American organization was well quantified, and it was substantiated that it was doable with reasonable risks.
- The track record and passion of the Indian organization for market leadership was apparent.
- These combined with the trust that the American team built were responsible for the successful partnership.

On the other hand, my experience with the Japanese team was slightly different. It took much longer to convince the Japanese, as they believe in team based decision-making, but once convinced, they undertake the project as their own, and coach and help the Indian organization to succeed.

Jukka Lehtela

The Indian process of negotiation is itself quite different. If you negotiate with Americans, they have quality and money as two parameters and the tradeoff of the two is discussed. Indian tradeoffs are wider — education and salary — if you can give them education as a perk, then it can be a valuable tradeoff. Indians like to develop themselves.

Negotiations with the government are another story. While choosing our destination, we were keen to locate ourselves where the local government has as much power as the central government, and would not change rules in coming years. I was looking for a stable government and some tax exemptions as well. When the Tamil Nadu Government saw how many thousands of people we were planning to employ, they were open to co-operation and negotiation. We confirmed Chennai. Indian bureaucrats are very smart people, who see the future of the economy.

It's a fact...

We recognized upfront that our leadership team would need to be involved in a lot of the details of the building design and construction to properly build a facility that served the city of Chennai, but conformed to the safety and operational standards of the rest of the world. Climate control was a frequent topic of discussion, due to the hot and humid climate in the area. We spent days discussing how to provide comfortable and dependable air-conditioning for the facility. Our partner was surprised that we required all of the restrooms to be air-conditioned, as well as the rest of the building. Upon completion, the building owner put my name on the restroom doors to assure the occupants that this had been my idea! We all had a good laugh!

– Sherry Murphree

Zia Mody

While negotiating with an American:

a. He/She wants the document to reflect certainty, he doesn't want too many provisos, so again, stick to the bottom line approach.

b. He/She wants to ensure he gets what he signs up for, and sometimes this is very difficult to assure him. This is because Indians often see a signed document as a starting position, and the Americans see it as the end of very expensive negotiations.

c. He/She asks, "What is the quality of my counterpart? Are these good industrial houses? Will they let me down? Will they stick to quality? Will I have trouble with the Foreign Corrupt Practices Act? Will I have compliance issues, because I am partnering with them?"

This reputational anxiety of the American partners is key. So have your document reflect and speak to these three points for a negotiation to go well.

While negotiating with Indians on the other hand:

a. They like the document to have as much room for maneuvering as possible.

b. They would like to have options embedded in the document. They, rightly, want the best of all worlds — no downside, all upside.

c. They negotiate hard, and are far more sophisticated than they were earlier. They now look to professionals, like us, more and more, and understand that not getting good advice in the beginning is not worth the problems they encounter later.

d. Signing on the dotted line is carefully weighed before taking action.

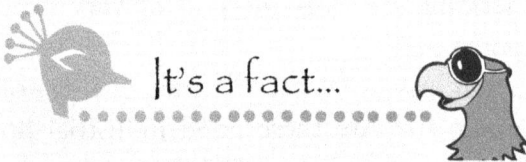

It's a fact...

We were looking for where we could set up our factory. The Tamil Nadu Government made a lot of promises, but also kept its word. When they heard we had selected the State, they acted fast with the paper work. It took two hours for the correct decision maker to come, and then they forged ahead, brought out a letter of intent, and seeing our need to sign off, stayed up all night to complete the MOU signing. Finally, we finished at 1 o' clock at night and they woke up various people in power to sign the agreement. The Nokia plan was set, and in six months, we built a state-of-the-art plant which produced cell phones. We went on to become the Number 1 MNC in India that year!

– Jukka Lehtela

When I give an answer, I sometimes have to change it later on. How do I re-open a topic and discuss?

Zia Mody

The best way to do this, as always, is to be transparent. Preface your conversation with clear remarks. I made a point the other day and my client disagreed, so I had to go back, and that's not the best way to do it. But what I had to do was say, "I told you this, and it was under the following assumptions. These are the new discussions I have now had, and this is the reason why my client wants to change his position." The point is not to put it cagily, or say, "Oh you misheard" or "Did I say that? I actually meant to say this"; "Actually, I never said it was gold, I always said it was silver, you thought it was gold" etc. That way, the other person will think you are dishonest. But, if you say "I thought it was gold for these reasons, but for (whatever the reasons are) which I am now articulating, it is silver, and I apologize for this disconnect, but, it is better we get on to the same page quickly and move forward."

Is there a guideline for me to know when I should play 'hard ball' and when I need to be patient in negotiations?

Zia Mody

With Indians you always have to be patient! They

tend to have a higher number of meetings. You need to get firm on both sides of the table, if after a certain set of meetings, positions have not changed. If it is a deal breaker for one side or the other, then, you certainly have to be able to say, not necessarily in an abrasive way, "Look this is a breaking point, lets huddle, and either, we achieve something or we stop and call it a day." Then, of course, it goes back to who blinks first.

Please give us a story on a successful deal you concluded.

Krishna Kumar

Starbucks was a great deal and I am so glad to have spearheaded it along with Mr. Ratan Tata. Howard Schulz, founder of Starbucks, became a good friend at the end of it. He flew to India and went straight to Coorg, where Tata has coffee plantations, and he fell in love with the operations and people, and liked what we were doing for labourers and their families. When he came back to Bombay, we met and I advised him that the right partner would be Tata Coffee, but Howard wanted to partner with Tata Global Beverages. I made it very clear that we didn't want to be in a position of merely facilitating an entry for Starbucks to India. We wanted to be a true partner.

We were not going to be open to all decisions being taken elsewhere with us playing the role of mere agents. Mr. Ratan Tata and I were very clear that this was a fifty-fifty partnership.

He understood we were not in the position that maybe smaller companies were.

Next Howard offered to call it Tata Starbucks. We didn't want names changed. We always take joint decisions when we partner with someone. The Chairman, in this case, me, was an Indian. We had our own scheme of things. We respected what they stood for and didn't expect a name change, in the same way they respected us. The deal was struck with shared values as a win-win for both sides.

NourishCo was also an equal partnership, which we negotiated with Ms. Indra Nooyi of PepsiCo. It makes Nutrient Water, an innovative product that aims to provide micronutrients, apart from Tata Water Plus, Tata Gluco Plus, and other hydrating solutions, which are distributed in India and abroad. Intense R&D was done all over the world for this.

It's a fact...

We acquired a thirty per cent stake in Vitamin Water from the US. I met the energetic Manhattan entrepreneur Darius Bikoff, who had come up with the idea of injecting vitamins into water for health. Knowing the trend for health in the world, we decided to acquire a thirty per cent stake by investing 677 million dollars into that enterprise. It was not making profit at that time, but Bikoff's idea was a brilliant one. It had superb management; it became a preferred drink for active people. So this way we added to our group — tea, coffee, beverages and even Himalayan mineral water. Our customers were world over. A global mind-set is the only way to go. Coke became interested in acquiring that company, and as minority shareholders, we were open to going along with the 4.5 billion deal, of which we received 1.2 billion, making a net profit of 500 million in a month's time. Being a part of this deal got us looking at what was going on in the American marketplace.

— Krishna Kumar

How do we show that price is less important to us than relationship and that we want to do business for the long term?

Sherry Murphree

Relationships are important for Americans, as well, but, it may not be on the top of the priority list in negotiating. Some things are important to consider, like being available in emergencies to deliver goods and services on time, and the quality of the product or service. Of course, some people may take the easy way out and focus solely on price.

We need to discuss what is important, quantifying skills and reputation, and the entire package. That said, companies may be looking for alternative partners to be sure that the value is worth what we get for our relationship.

It's a fact...

Sometimes you have to play hard ball in India. I was invited to make a presentation at a function. And because the top government official was coming, they were collecting everybody's phone as a security measure. A total of 200 phones were collected. When I showed up at the door, they said I had to give them my phone, but I didn't want to part with it. So, I simply said, "No, sorry. I'm not going to do the presentation." Then they let me carry my phone! If you walk away from a negotiation table — they will call you back. It is an all or nothing kind of negotiation which works well in India.

– Jukka Lehtela

CHAPTER 8

COMMUNICATION STYLES

It is not just what you say, but, also, how you say things that matters. This chapter gives insights into the nuances of effective multi-cultural business communications, both in India and from remote locations in virtual business scenarios. The power of the word, balanced with the magic of silence, can make a difference to the bottom line of a business and can hasten the journey towards business goals. The most important things to say can also be the easiest things not to say, unless we realize their importance. This section has some clear pointers on communicating like a global citizen.

Getting to the point
Photo: Ben Bowling, USA

What are the new global communication standards required to effectively do business in today's India?

Sherry Murphree

Indians speak good English. However, sometimes each side was using words not clearly understood by the other. For example, I was in a meeting and the group kept talking about *'preponing'* some of the activity. I had to ask, "What are you talking about?" and then found that this meant advancing the activity. When Indians work with Americans, they also need to be sure they understand what is being said as we use a lot of Americanisms that originated in our sports terminology. Some Americans find the Indian English accent difficult to understand. We can be intolerant and arrogant in America, and some people were complaining that they couldn't understand what their Indian counterpart was saying, while their Indian counterparts found the American speed of speech hard to get used to, as well. We tried to be fair and set expectations both ways.

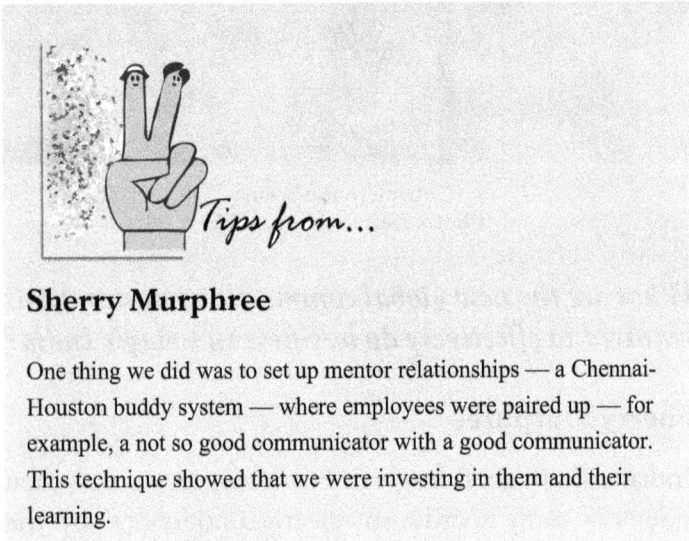

Tips from...

Sherry Murphree

One thing we did was to set up mentor relationships — a Chennai-Houston buddy system — where employees were paired up — for example, a not so good communicator with a good communicator. This technique showed that we were investing in them and their learning.

Kirthiga Reddy

I have had experience when the deal was off, because a 6 p.m. time zone deadline was not clarified — whether it was 6 p.m. Indian time or US time. Also, another time — 6 p.m. Indian time comes, and something has happened to delay it, then it is 8 p.m. or 10 p.m. Then, they are like, "Anyway, it is so late and I might as well send it tomorrow morning. Anyway it is not going to matter." But, there is no communication about this. It is incredible how we underestimate accountability, clear communication, and clear expectation setting. It does matter to reinforce trust with every little communication you carry out and goal you achieve.

Or you will be working cross border and having a discussion, and it is 11 p.m. or 12 midnight and you fall asleep. Can you, at least, let the other person know, "It is 11 p.m. here, and I am going to be logging off in a half an hour. If there is anything you need, do let me know." That way, the other person is not wondering what just happened, as there is complete silence from the other end. Small things go a long way and these things make or break a person's career.

Phil Spender

The power is shifting. Rich nations are getting poorer and the BRIC nations are getting richer. Dialogue is the key. Trading will lead to less war. If other nations want to take advantage of what India has to offer, they have to help many more numbers of people improve their lives. Debunk stereotypes and put yourself in the other's shoes, hold cultural dialogues, and profit will follow.

A lot of the trends that you see overseas are happening here in India and almost quicker than they did overseas, frankly. Car consumer behaviour — of seeing the car as an extension of one's personality — is happening and the numbers in India are mind boggling. It is a nation with a robust workforce and consumers. They can help the rest of the world win.

Tips from...

Sherry Murphree

People may skip starting an email with 'Dear' these days, and that's not rude, it just saves time.

As Americans and Indians may not be able to tell if it is a man or a woman writing the emails going by name alone, do write Mr. or Ms. In brackets when you sign off, to indicate gender.

A punchy subject line will ensure that an email is opened, so take time to frame it.

Indians seem to always have additional personal information on each other, and form a connection in minutes. How can I develop this advantage, or leverage their strength?

Krishna Kumar

Wish I could say there was a way to imbibe this. We should be aware of this reality that culture rules human beings very strongly. It is indeed a dimension of Indian culture to strike a chord easily, we can develop this strength in our teams, and we should also be open to multi-cultural friendships.

Is researching your expat business guests a good thing for preparation?

Kirthiga Reddy

Absolutely, and nowadays with capabilities like Facebook, you can empower yourself with knowledge; you don't go into a meeting without specific information. You do not write a generic email saying, "Hi, can I have a meeting." Find out what is going on in their life and craft a real message. It is unbelievable how often people don't do that, and actually it is so simple. For example, you wrote me about Sheryl's visit and interest in India, and then asked if I would participate in this book; it piqued my interest, as I was checking Facebook between flights, and here I am.

I apply that to a client presentation as well; you never go to a client with a vanilla presentation, saying this is what you have. To me, if it doesn't have some logo, or some product of theirs, where it shows you put some thought into what their needs are and how we can solve them, then, I don't even go there. So research is a cheap tool that people should definitely use.

With virtual teams, so much of the feedback we give is lost, how do we articulate it?

Kirthiga Reddy

Constructive feedback is hard to give when you are face to face. I have found that, across the ocean, it gets even more muted. A manager would tell me, "I am furious with this person." You would read the written feedback, however, and would have no clue that this person is furious with the other one. My advice across the globe has been — if you have constructive feedback and you think the decibel level has to be at 10, try doing it at a 100. That's the only way you will be able to get the message across. As a leader, it is your responsibility to give constructive feedback and I have seen so many instances where there's just been an escalation of confusion. The team in India would be thinking, "Why am I not being entrusted by them to take on work?" and on the American side, they are thinking, "Why aren't they taking on more work?" Clarity of communication is crucial. Regular, frequent, succinct messaging of what each side wants is needed.

Tips from...

Stuart Milne

In India it's much easier to manage than in Asian countries like China or Japan, as it is informal here and there is no language barrier. An American will have to listen more though, and pick up the cues here, be attuned to what someone is telling you, as he may not tell you verbally.

Why should I escalate delays and bad news if I feel it might get solved?

Stuart Milne

The inclination to keep bad news from the boss is observable in India, but it is a universal tendency and a dangerous way to manage things.

It is better to state the bad news the moment you have it, as it can perhaps be fixed at that point with some help from outside. Also, usually, bad things get worse, so you don't want to tell your boss until weeks later, when it might have doubled in size.

I do that with my boss — "These three things are going on and we are working on fixing them, but they may come up as issues later on." And when I have solved it, I update him, even today.

Tips from...

Kirthiga Reddy

I would like to say something on concise communication. 'Do you have your elevator pitch ready?' That is a crisp message about who you are and what you do, delivered in under a minute so that, even if you have only that amount of time on an elevator with someone that matters, you can come across sensible and he or she will want to connect with you. In India, we do have trouble with concise communication. We also have a problem over generalizing, and getting to the point and making things clear. You can't invest enough on communication. I find it is a lifelong improvement curve. Every six-month period, I make an investment in myself to up my communication skills, from whatever level it is at, to the next one.

What SMSs, voice, teleconference, videoconference, email protocol would you advise for Indians?

Jukka Lehtela

My advice for communication is to use face-to-face, email, or text equally carefully. Write full words, not shortcuts, use commas and full stops, with 'Dear' and such salutations — just like a business communication. For video conferences, we had a team in India and a group in China and, they were all able to see and listen, but after fifteen minutes I realized it was not working. Sometimes smaller teams communicate better. So I stopped the group video conferences, and suggested one-to-one communication for the next video conference. That way people can understand each other really well. It becomes a waste of time if too many people are involved. It works well as a buddy system and people bond very well, even virtually.

Research says good first impressions are formed fifty-five per cent by appearance, thirty-eight per cent by the way you speak, seven per cent by how you craft your message. What is your advice to prepare for this?

Kirthiga Reddy

Your message is key. There is a lot of thought that body

language, tone and appearance matter. My take is — unless you have substance, the rest doesn't matter and I give up on you. A speech can be powerful just because of the content, but if you are a fantastic speaker with no content, it can be a vacuum. I do agree that the way you come across, the way you project yourself, makes a big difference. It will give a short term initial impression; but content is needed for the long term. And on the flip side, if you are shoddily dressed, slouched over, it also takes people a longer time to give you that room and mind to share your ideas.

CHAPTER 9

INDIA IMPACT

Electrifying the world
Photo: Greg Hamra, USA

What is your best memory of India?

Sherry Murphree

Two things — when our company first moved into our building, we had a ceremony where we brought in a Hindu priest, a Catholic priest, and a Muslim cleric to come and bless the building — everyone in unison celebrating something together. Nowhere, but in India, can we celebrate something like this.

Secondly, the kindness of Indian people is amazing. My secretary got up at 4 a.m., cooked for her family and then came to work. When I had some health problems, she decided to wake up at 3 a.m. to go to the temple to pray for me before she cooked. This was so touching. I was impressed by the simple kindness people had.

It's a fact...

We tried to think of everything and almost treated our Indian teams like children. We put them through a training programme on US business, culture and etiquette, and provided them lots of hand-holding and help once they landed in Texas. However, we maybe didn't set their expectations correctly.

We had housed them in an apartment block next door to the office building in Houston, and when it rained on Monday morning, all seventeen of them didn't show up at work, as they were waiting for someone to come and bring them umbrellas in the apartment which had none! This showed us we, also, had to balance out 'taking care' with 'independence building' of our teams. We also figured out pretty quickly that people who came to India with a driving license and started driving would get into a car accident in five minutes. So we ended up saying that Americans and Indians had to get more experience and training before they started driving in either country.

– Sherry Murphree

What would be the one most important ingredient to add into the making of a Global Citizen?

Shanker Annaswamy

Find ways to show that you CARE for the common objective of the team, COMMIT yourself to success and build CREDIBILITY by executing, time and again, the tasks that have been assigned to you. While it takes time and effort to gain credibility, you can lose the same very quickly with a single misstep. You are as good as your last accomplishment. So it is good to stay consistent and deliver.

What did you learn from India that you use to this day?

Sherry Murphree

I learned patience. From the Indian sense of time, which is measured in bigger increments than in the US, I learned to think of the long term, not just the very immediate short term. I also learned to value the relationships you build. Every day I still get a message from one of my friends from India, whereas, I hardly ever hear from people from my work in the US.

Jukka Lehtela

Summarizing all my good memories of India, one memory is the family day we held annually at Nokia. I was walking around and talking to the people when one of the girls stopped me and showed me a photo of her family and told me how I had made a difference in her life. This was real positive feedback! It was nice to know that one operator's life had turned around by working at Nokia! I still try to do the best for people.

Stuart Milne

Knowing the family dynamics of the person you are

working with is very important in India, and should be as important anywhere else, but it isn't. I have learned it and appreciated it here, and I will do it a lot more, wherever I go next. It makes work meaningful.

Phil Spender

I am much more patient. I manage to get people to see the same picture. India teaches you a lot about getting people to a common vision and goals. I came to appreciate the lateral thinking of Indian professionals. I am full of respect for Indian minds. India taught me to manage teams better, I got noticed by my work there, and became Vice-President of Ford Motor Company.

David Sloan

That is a big question. I will make several points.

I think the whole issue of respect is paramount. There are advantages in some cases for the kind of hierarchy in Indian culture, and for deferring to this clear chain of command. In Western cultures, there is more of a propensity to try to circumvent bureaucracy in order to get ahead. It is much more difficult to do that in India.

In some cases, the work-family balance is probably better in India, instead of being wedded to the job as we can be in the west.

Also, because Indian culture is very diverse, Indians

are accustomed to dealing with people of different languages and backgrounds, so that Indians can go anywhere in world and adapt, compared to Americans, who are more culturally homogeneous.

It is important for Indians to realize that in the US, there are more distinctly different corporate cultures than in Indian companies. The IBM corporate culture, for instance, or at least the old IBM culture, was a very specific one, compared to, say the culture at Facebook, for example (leaders of both those companies have spoken elsewhere in this book). Indians working with US firms need to understand the specific corporate culture they plan to enter.

It's a fact...

Can you imagine, Ford did not have a design standard for a horn, till India came along! Honking is very much a part of the culture and India became a centre of excellence for horn development in the world. Durability and longevity in horns — improvements which are now used globally — India was at the forefront of them.

– Phil Spender

How has India made an impact on your company and vice-versa?

Kirthiga Reddy

I have two stories to tell.

The first is about diversity. Diversity is at the core of India, not just gender but linguistic, cultural and economic diversity. We address all those needs inclusively, as this country gives you the opportunity to do so. Facebook fills such a basic human need to share and connect, that it is pretty universal. At Facebook we take a country-level customization and product perspective. In India, we support nine different languages on the mobile device, and ten on a desktop. We support feature phones. People think of us as a metro smart phone phenomenon, but sixty-six per cent of our mobile base use Facebook. Now we have over 100 million people using Facebook in India. Eighty-four per cent use it from a mobile device. Sixty-six per cent of those are feature phones, and the rest are smart phones. There is within that a very strong distribution of metros as well as non-metros and smaller tier 2 or tier 3 towns. So, India offers growth and opportunities beyond people's imagination, if you get it right with product and strategy for this market.

The second is my favorite Facebook story. There was a farmer in Sangli. Turmeric prices were dropping.

He used Facebook to rally 26,000 farmers across the country; and they figured out a strategy for the supply-demand equation and fixed the issue. Impact in India can be two-fold: social and economic.

CHAPTER 10

BEING A GLOBAL CITIZEN

In the 21st century, we are no longer confined by barriers, borders, or walls that separate us from one another. Today, cell phones, the social media, the internet, the 24-hour news cycle, and our economic interdependence, all make us, whether we like it or not, instant global citizens. These are exciting times! India and America are intertwined in a myriad ways that unite us and make us interdependent. With the new national leadership in India and the geopolitical shifts on the planet, India and the United States will, of necessity, now need to work closely with each other. With that increased virtual and geopolitical proximity comes responsibility. There is no excuse for any of us sitting comfortably isolated in our particular demographic of place, gender, education, nation, or ethnicity. To survive today, we must all adjust to this global 'new normal' or be left behind.

That is the reason we wrote this book and why we began working in the field of global understanding and cross-cultural competence twenty years ago. We believe that adjusting oneself to become global takes some effort and time. This adjustment means being open to experiences, holding non-ethnocentric attitudes, self-monitoring, and attempting to understand differences. It takes practice and study. The global person accepts multiple perspectives, allows for compromise, is flexible and willing to negotiate solutions that are acceptable, and incorporates cultural diversity into his/her daily life.

Communication is the key to this learning. Asking the right questions and listening to diverse views brings increased understanding and an ability to function on this culturally rich and diverse planet. Our belief is that by utilizing the best practices from each culture, one can arrive at a higher level of global functioning that works in today's world. By asking real questions that we heard from business Americans and Indians over these years, of some of today's business leaders, we have given you some insights into how a global person might do business in the new India.

We are sure you will have picked up some cues as to how to make your business more internationally successful. Continuing to sift through conflicting information to find the best solutions to business goals and issues will produce a fully functioning, internationally-savvy business model that all of us will begin to adopt. Ask appropriate questions, and adjust your behaviour to accommodate optimal multi-cultural productivity. In this evolution toward a globally adjusted world, all of us are players. We are all somewhere along this learning curve, and we will continue to need to learn, listen, adjust and change. We will have to discard old ethnocentric ways of working that hinder collaboration. We will have to reject attitudes that are stagnant or judgmental of others, in exchange for attitudes that are fluid and open to new ways of working together. At the same time, we should teach each other our cherished cultural traditions, and honor and respect that which is very different, utilizing the best of each culture, and at the same time finding a middle road to collaboration that allows us to work and live together.

There is an ancient Indian saying, which says all learnings in life come from four quarters:

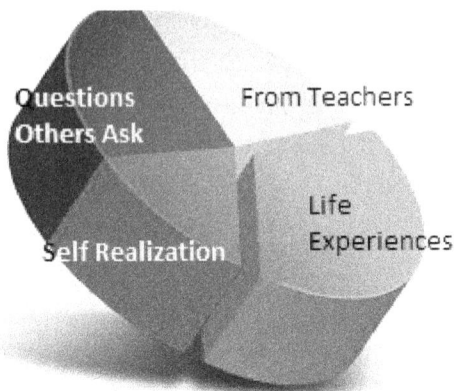

- *One quarter you learn from a teacher, which we hope this book will be.*
- *A second quarter you learn from questions others ask, which again, we hope these questions have done*
- *A third quarter comes from your own reflection, which we hope you will do — applying the learnings of this book to your specific life situations.*
- *A final quarter comes from life experiences, which we hope will teach you well.*

For after all, what matters is what you do with what you know.

Balancing Act

As this image of India's favourite monkey God Hanuman, known for his skilled communication shows, it is a fine balancing act.

Go forward into the world with external and internal customers balanced on both your shoulders. American and Indian balanced on both sides, and personal and professional balanced as well.

May your communication be measured, pleasant, thoughtful, clear, and only what is necessary.

Globally adjust as you go, for the world belongs to Indo-US collaborators, who are willing and ready to meet in the middle.

The future is here
Photo: Ninna Marie Hogedal, Denmark

Takeaways from the book

- *Respect is paramount.*
- *Treat others as you want to be treated.*
- *Win over the American by presenting facts and data, and walking the talk.*
- *Win over the Indian by presenting the bigger picture and removing road blocks for him or her to succeed.*
- *Continue to adjust and grow your international skill base.*

- *Debunk stereotypes and put yourself in the other's shoes, hold cultural dialogues, and profit will follow.*
- *'One-on-one Communication', whether in person or virtually, works best and builds better bonds among work colleagues.*
- *Learning from the example of other global teams is key to making Indian-expat teams work. Hire people with a global view and experience.*
- *Knowing the family dynamics of the person you are working with is very important in India. It makes work meaningful.*
- *Develop a new participative mind-set and be aware you are now orbiting a different world, reaching out across world operations to global customers.*
- *In a global world, where different backgrounds are coming into the foreground, it is crucial to address offensive behaviour upfront, and iron out differences one on one, so that the rest of the time can be spent on doing core business.*
- *Realize that you are part of something bigger. Your actions can contribute to a much vaster platform, because we are all living in an interconnected world. Humanity is going to benefit from your global footprint, as you contribute to building community in all the places you serve.*
- *Have a picture of the vision of the company and where it can go, connecting the dots between the organizational goals. Also have your own ideas and ask and share them. Don't go in there passively and say I want to be part of the bigger picture!*

- *Contracts and relationships have different connotations in the two cultures. To an American, signing the contract is the final step in a long and expensive process. Once it is done, he expects it to be followed to the last letter (and comma, semi-colon and full stop).*

- *An Indian sees the signing of the contract as but one step in a long-term relationship, which will see much chopping and changing as the relationship progresses. To an Indian, the contract is only a broad framework to work with. The details have yet to be worked out.*

- *Make a commitment to '**Make it In India**'. Make it work with India. With an underlying commitment to respect for all parties, work to educate and train managers and employees both in the US and in India about how the other culture works, and how to co-operate on a level playing field. Starting with practical small things like switching between both time zones for alternate virtual meetings, right up to ensuring that all voices are heard.*

- *The bottom line in negotiating — Understand the other's mindset, and Be Prepared!*

ACKNOWLEDGEMENTS

Our thanks and gratitude to all those who helped make this book a reality:

- Mr Narayana Murthy for his inspiring Foreword to our book.
- All the eleven CEOs interviewed in the book who gave so willingly of their time and stories.
- Ravi Venkatesan, David Sloan and Shanker Annaswamy for sifting through early questions and guiding us.
- Susan Philip for being our most resourceful editorial co-ordinator, helping us stay on track, and being a guiding light for this project.
- Shanti Puducheri for providing so many questions asked by our workshop participants over the years from our training department.
- Vijay Puducheri for selecting some good questions from a Non-resident Indian angle.

Acknowledgements

- Thank you to Lalitha Thyagarajan, our talented artist, who created Indo-US icons so cleverly to use throughout the book and for creating multiple cover designs for the book before hitting on this final apt and attractive one you see now.

- Global Adjustments Team members Markus Reichert and Premkumar for being our technical whizkids and Shobana Sairaj Kumar for coordinating the interviews.

- We express our sincere thanks to Basia Kruzewska, Brigitte Rhodius, Emma Horne, Ben Bowling and Diana Grieger who gave us permission to use their images in the book. Every effort was made to contact Sue Taylor, Ninna Marie Hogedal, Paul Fejer, Greg Hamra, Emmanuel Mancion, Yngve Andersson and Elena Eder to obtain their permission to use their images as well. But, we were unable to touch base with them. We owe them our sincere thanks as well.

- Karthik, our Editor on the Tata Westland team, along with Krishna Kumar, Sudha and Gautam for their patient help and making this book a reality.

- Our husbands, K S Manian and Jim Huskey for guiding and mentoring our book in New York City, and our lives in general.

It's an Interconnected World beneath the mask – Namaste
Photo: Elena Eder, Germany